THE M.C.C. CRICKET COACHING BOOK

Gary Sobers driving: poise and power

THE M.C.C.
CRICKET COACHING
BOOK

Published officially for
The M.C.C. by
WILLIAM HEINEMANN LTD

William Heinemann Ltd
LONDON   MELBOURNE   TORONTO
CAPE TOWN   AUCKLAND

First published by Naldrett Press Ltd
April 1952
Reprinted 1952, 1954
Second edition published by the Naldrett Press Ltd
in association with the World's Work (1913) Ltd 1955
Reprinted 1957, 1959
Third edition published by William Heinemann Ltd 1962
Reprinted 1965, 1968 1972, 1974

434 46001 X

Made and printed in Great Britain by
Morrison and Gibb Limited
London and Edinburgh

Contents

		Page
THE SPIRIT OF THE GAME	. . . .	1
1 FIELDING	. . . .	3
2 WICKET-KEEPING	. . . . .	21
3 BOWLING	. . . . . .	30
4 BATTING	. . . . . .	70
5 CAPTAINCY	. . . . . .	110
6 LEARNING BY WATCHING	. . . .	117
7 NET PRACTICE	. . . . .	122
8 GROUP COACHING—WHY AND HOW	. . .	126
9 THE CHOICE AND CARE OF EQUIPMENT	. .	145
10 GROUNDS AND PITCHES	. . . .	149

List of Illustrations

FIELDING

Peter Parfitt, 16a, 16b, 16c
Tony Lock, 16d
England slips, 16d

BOWLING

Maurice Tate, 32a
Ray Lindwall, 32b
Harold Larwood, 32c
Fred Truman, 32d
Alec Bedser, 40a

C. V. Grimmett, 40b
Jim Laker, 40b
Richie Benaud, 48a
Hedley Verity, 48b, 48c
Pat Pocock, 48d

BATTING

Gary Sobers, frontispiece

Peter May, 80a, 96a
Colin Cowdrey, 80a, 80c, 96b
W. G. Grace, 80b
Jack Hobbs, 80d
V. T. Trumper, 88a
Barry Richards, 88a

Wally Hammond, 88b
Len Hutton, 88b
Don Bradman, 96a, 104a
Geoffrey Boycott, 96c
Clive Lloyd, 96d
Lindsay Hassett, 96d

Denis Compton, 104b

WICKET-KEEPING

Alan Knott, 128a

Godfrey Evans, 128b

GROUP COACHING, 128c, 128d

The drawings specially made for this edition of the book are the work of Mr Bruce Drysdale. Thanks are also due to Mr Peter May, Mr Colin Cowdrey, and Mr Peter Parfitt for their co-operation over some of the photographs.

Foreword

The first edition of this book was published in 1952 and as the then President of M.C.C., Mr W. Findlay, said in his foreword, it represented the first official attempt by the Club to review the whole field of the game's technique. The M.C.C. Youth Cricket Association, who were responsible for its production, have been greatly encouraged not only by its sale, amounting now to nearly 40,000 copies and extending over every part of the world where the game is played, but by the continual endorsement of its tenets on the coaching courses organized by the Association at Lilleshall and by its affiliated County Associations throughout the country, an endorsement covering as wide a field as Test match cricketers of long coaching experience and enthusiastic schoolmasters struggling with the problems of space and numbers in the Secondary Modern schools.

The problems of the coach inevitably differ according to the conditions under which he has to work. It is comparatively easy to 'take a net' of three or four promising cricketers on a true turf pitch, but it is a very different thing to try to initiate into the game twenty or thirty real beginners on an asphalt playground. This, however, is the challenging task with which a great many coaches are faced, and it is to help them that the technique of Group Coaching, described in Chapter 8, was evolved.

But though the first object of this book is to suggest to the coach what to teach and how to teach it, it is hoped that it may also appeal to the young cricketer who is keen to know what to learn and how to apply it, and even perhaps to the more mature player who may be reminded by it of things he has forgotten or find old truths presented, perhaps, in a fresh light.

An attempt has been made by the use of heavy type to emphasize the essentials, whether for the coach or for the boy, in each department of the game, and to elucidate them by photographs and drawings together with the notes that accompany them.

Before embarking on the new edition of this book, the Association convened a conference comprising both contemporary players and county coaches, many of them of high distinction, to review the whole text in the light of their experience over the last eight years. In two long days of debate, many suggestions were made and as a result of these, we hope that this book may be more helpful both to the coach and the young cricketer. There is also a completely new set of drawings and diagrams and many new photographs covering a more contemporary generation of players. Despite these innovations, it is interesting to note that in no single instance has there been disagreement on any of the basic principles laid down in the original edition.

Young cricketers will, and of course should, as they grow up, develop on individual lines according to their natural gifts of eye and reaction, their physique, their temperament and their character: perhaps the hardest of all problems for the coach is to know 'what to leave alone' and the last thing he should hope to do is to turn out players on a uniform and unimaginative pattern. Criticism has at times been voiced that we do just this, with the accent basically on defence. We invite such cricketers to study the text of this book: still better, let them come to a M.C.C. course and see for themselves; in text and in practice they will find that we preach 'attack' in every department of the game. If, however, such attack is to be successfully initiated, still more sustained, there are basic techniques which have to be mastered and which in fact even the greatest players of all generations have observed far more than they have disregarded.

But a good cricket coach must be able to do something more than demonstrate and teach technique: he must get to know his boys as individuals and, by his enthusiasm and encouragement, make them feel that he really cares about their success and that this game which he is trying to help them to play is not only something to be enjoyed, but something that in its traditions, values, and comradeship can strengthen and enrich the fabric of their lives.

To all those who out of their love of the game have helped in the making of this book, the Committee of the M.C.C. wish to express their grateful thanks, and in particular to Mr G. O. Allen and Mr H. P. Crabtree.

H. S. Altham.

CHAIRMAN, M.C.C. YOUTH
CRICKET ASSOCIATION

The Spirit of the Game

Cricket is, in a sense, warfare in miniature and a cricket match should be fought out by both sides with all the resources of spirit and technique at their command. At the same time it should always be a recreation, a game to be played not only according to written laws but in harmony with an unwritten code of chivalry and good temper.

A cricket team should feel that they are playing with, as well as against, their opponents. The home side should remember that they are hosts, the visitors that they are guests, and both should realize that the true greatness of the game lies in combat and comradeship combined.

Pursued in such a spirit, victory, and nothing short of victory, should be the object of both teams from the first over of the match. The bowlers and fielders of the one, the batsmen of the other, should go on to the field determined to attack and to go on attacking until they are really forced to fall back on defence, and even then to resume the offensive directly the balance of the game permits.

It would seem that of recent years this instinct for attack has tended to give place to a premature concern with defence in which the batsman's chief aim is to stay at the wicket rather than to make runs and the bowler's is to keep down the rate of run-getting rather than to get wickets. With the resulting development of defensive technique in batting, bowling and field-placing the game is in danger of becoming less vital and less enjoyable for players and spectators alike.

The coaches of today can do cricket no greater service than by helping the cricketers of the future to recapture the spirit and the armoury of attack: only so can they win from the game the best that it has to give them.

In no other game perhaps is the individual and his team so closely integrated. One man can virtually win a match, not necessarily by technical skill, but by intelligence, concentration and character: one man can lose it by a failure in those qualities. Conversely the morale of each member of an eleven can be largely built up and sustained by the atmosphere of the whole. Unity of purpose and belief in each other is a tremendous asset in cricket, and it is usually possible to sense it by watching a team take the field or listening to them talk as they sit and watch the game from the pavilion. It was not by hazard that one of the most famous of amateur cricket clubs called itself 'The Band of Brothers'.

1

Nor does any other game expose a player to a more varied or exacting trial. It can be a lonely and formidable experience to walk out, perhaps after an agonizing wait, to bat at the crisis of a school match, possibly to face a fast bowler on a fiery pitch, or a spinner on a sticky one: formidable too to stand under a high catch knowing that to miss it may cost the game. Bowler and fielder alike may often towards the end of a hard day have 'to force their heart and nerve and sinew to serve their turn long after they are gone'.

There are also the less obvious but more insidious trials of failure and success: the greatest players will have spells when nothing will go right; then comes the test of still keeping cheerful and finding some consolation in the success of others: and if fortune smiles for a time and the game seems easy and all men speak well of him, the true cricketer will remember to keep a modest mind as well as a straight bat.

1

Fielding

To stop, to catch and to throw a ball are the easiest and most natural of cricket activities. **No boy – or man – who is not prepared to do his best to become a good fielder has really the right to call himself a cricketer.** For as fielder, more even than as batsman or bowler, he is a member of a team and can not only determine the result of a game by a catch, a run-out or a saved boundary, but, as long as he is on the field, can inspire or depress his fellows by example. Nothing reveals more clearly the spirit of a school team, the leadership of its captain and the inspiration of its coach than the quality of that team's fielding: moreover, fine fielding not only constitutes an immense reinforcement to its bowlers but presents to the opposing batsmen a formidable front, psychological as well as physical.

Best of all, it will prove a real reinforcement of confidence and loyalty in the team itself. There is all the difference in the world between a school team that just 'takes the field' and one that, on losing the toss on a hot day, goes out to field meaning to enjoy itself and to win credit into the bargain.

Perhaps the most important of all cricket truths which a coach can instil is that fielding is fun and infinitely more fun if everyone tries.

THE BASIC TECHNIQUE

Of course boys differ widely in physical co-ordination and what is easy and natural to one can only be achieved through long and determined practice by another: but there is really no reason why any school team should field badly, provided they are keen enough, practise enough, and their practice is wisely and enthusiastically directed.

Good fielding calls for quick starting, quick stooping and balance. These can, without doubt, be stimulated by activity exercises in the gymnasium or out in the open, during the winter as well as in the season: any competent P.E. Teacher will, if consulted, be able to provide the right type of exercises and nothing is more certain in cricket than that such an investment will pay a dividend.

But, of course, the major part of the job has to be done out in the open and with a ball.

DEFENSIVE FIELDING

The mental attitude of all fielders must be aggressive but, as in batting, their attack must be based on a sound technique of defence. Their first job is to stop the ball.

Quick starting

To stop a ball a fielder must first get to it, and this means he must be able to start at the earliest possible moment: we will say, directly he has sighted the line of the stroke, for only experience will enable him to anticipate it and even then he may sometimes be wrong.

For quick starting he must:

(i) **Watch the batsman** (unless he is first-slip or leg-slip when he will watch the ball from the bowler's hand).

(ii) **Be balanced** on the balls of both feet with body slightly stooped at the waist and knees, and with hands hanging loosely at the ready in front of him.

(iii) **Be concentrated** in mind, expecting each ball to be played to **him**.

Stopping the ball

He must:

(i) Get on to the line of the ball as quickly as possible.

(ii) Get down early and stay down.

(iii) Watch the ball with complete concentration until it is safely in his hands.

There are two accepted positions for receiving the ball in defensive fielding.

(a) Orthodox position

The fielder is facing full down the line of the ball with knees well bent, seat well down, and the fingers of both hands touching the ground to form the base of a triangle in which his closed heels are the apex; his head should not be much more than a foot above his hands and his eyes glued to the ball as it comes towards him (Fig. 1a).

(b) The Long Barrier position

The fielder turns sideways to the line of the ball, dropping on his left knee so that his left leg and his body present a maximum barrier to the ball. His hands will be down to receive the ball in front of his left thigh, and his head directly over them and fully turned so that he watches the ball into them with both eyes level (Fig. 1b).

Fig. 1a.
Defence:
head right down watching
the ball into the hands

Fig. 1b.
Defence:
the long barrier position:
right foot, with left knee
overlapping, at right-angles
to line of ball: head directly
over hands

OFFENSIVE FIELDING

So far we have been concerned with the basic technique of defensive fielding: but there is an offensive technique as well, at which every boy must aim if he aspires to be a real fielder. In this the object is to receive the ball in such a position that the throw-in can follow immediately, indeed can almost be regarded as the last phase of a single process.

In attack the fielder must:

(i) **Intercept the line of the ball as early as possible:** this means moving not only on to it but in to it.

(ii) **Get sideways to the line** with the left foot carried rather away from the right (Fig. 2a).

(iii) **Bend both hips and knees** so that the head can come and stay down over, or just in front of, the right knee.

(iv) **Receive the ball in both hands just in front of the right foot,** and with the weight of the body on that foot (Fig. 2b).

For the maximum speed of return, he will have to risk using one hand and aim to pick up the ball just in front of his right foot. By so doing, he

Fig. 2a.
Attack:
the body in an accelerated approach has turned sideways, with the right foot in the final stride landing at right-angles to the line of the ball

Fig. 2b.
Attack:
the hands are down to receive the ball just in front of the right toe: head and eyes directly above point of interception

will be able, without further adjustment of feet or body, to begin the mechanism of the throw.

But this is a refinement of the basic technique of fielding and should not be taught until the essentials are mastered; even then it will probably be followed with success only by the naturally gifted and well-co-ordinated boy. In either practice the essence of safe fielding is that the head should get down on to the line of focus and then be kept still so as to watch the ball right into the hands.

Late stooping, snatching and looking up early are capital crimes.

Throwing

Fast and accurate throwing is the spearhead of aggressive fielding: the team that can command it will not only make the most of any chance of running batsmen out, but will also be slowing down their rate of run-getting by the threat of that fate.

Though really fine throwing demands special flexibility of wrist, elbow and shoulder, practically any boy can, if he will only practise, learn to throw adequately: the more he practises, the more he may hope to attain speed and accuracy as well.

The essence of a good throw is that of cracking a whip, i.e. the impulsive straightening of the arm from the elbow reinforced by the forward flick of the wrist. Small boys can practise this by themselves by bouncing a tennis or solid rubber ball and be encouraged by competition in the height of the bounce.

The chief points in throwing technique are:
(i) The ball should be watched right into the hands and be under their full control before the arm begins to move back for the throw: it is fatal to look up too soon.
(ii) The feet should be as already described for the offensive fielding position, with the right foot at right angles to the intended line of the throw, the knee slightly bent and the weight fully back on this foot.
(iii) The right arm, with elbow bent and wrist cocked, should travel on a line straight back from the right shoulder. At the same time the left arm and hand should stretch out to point at the target (Fig. 2c).
(iv) The body and the head must at all costs be balanced and kept on the same plane. The eyes and mind should concentrate on the top of the wicket aimed at.
(v) The release: as the right arm comes through in the throw, the trunk pivots so that at the moment of release the chest is facing the target and the weight is fully on the left leg and braced against the left hip.
(vi) The follow-through: the right arm carries through straight down the line of the throw and the right leg will naturally follow suit: at the finish the trunk has completed its pivot and the right shoulder is pointing at the target (Fig. 2d).

Fig. 2c.
Attack:
poised for the throw:
eyes looking along the
left arm, which points
straight at the target:
weight just beginning
to be transferred to
the left foot

Fig. 2d. Attack: the follow-through. Full pivot of the trunk, led by head
and right arm, straight down the line of the ball

In the case of the really good thrower these movements will be as synchronized and rhythmical as in a first-class bowling action.

There can be no doubt that the straighter, i.e. the more vertical, the line on which the throwing arm moves, the greater the accuracy of direction. For sheer speed of return, especially from cover-point or third-man, the sideways, below the shoulder, throw is more effective but it is far more difficult to control in direction, for the margin of error in timing the release is far narrower. Coaches will be wise to stick to the safer, if slightly slower technique, though, of course, encouraging the really gifted fielders to experiment with and practise the refinements: the same is true of the pure under-hand wrist flick for fast return at very short range.

Catching

Quite as many catches are missed by faulty positioning or lack of balance in the catcher as by any failure of the hands to grip the ball.

Fig. 3. Catching: head steady and eyes on the line: hands well spread: the ball will be caught at about eye level

Fig. 4. Safe and sound: the arms and hands have 'given' with the ball

M.C.C.—2

The essentials of safe catching are:

(i) Do not move until you have sighted the ball, then:

(ii) Get on to the line quickly, be relaxed and keep your head still.

(iii) Really watch the ball all the way, e.g. try to sight its seam.

(iv) Make a wide but relaxed ' web ' of your hands and fingers: the ideal place to catch the ball is at the base of the fingers which then automatically close round it (Fig. 3).

(v) Try to catch the ball wherever possible at eye-level: it is impossible to re-focus a ball dropping past the eyes.

(vi) Let your hands 'give' with the ball (Fig. 4).

In catching the fast hit straight at his body, the fielder should move it slightly to one side or the other, thus making it possible for the hands to 'ride with the ball': in catching the ball at or above the level of his chin, the web of his hands will be pointing upwards.

FIELDING PRACTICE

Quite apart from anything that a coach may achieve by instruction and organized practice, boys can do a very great deal for themselves if only they are keen enough – or made keen enough – to keep on playing about with the ball and so learning 'ball sense'. Even a very small boy by himself can learn to stop and catch a ball by throwing it against a wall, and to throw it accurately by aiming at a target chalked on the wall. Similarly, the coach should encourage all his boys to keep practising among themselves when he is otherwise engaged, suggesting that they should follow the lines of organized practice and competition on which he is trying to train them.

Confidence is a great asset in fielding, and much harm can be done if in the early stages hands are bruised and the cricket ball becomes an object of dread rather than a focus of enjoyment. For that reason, especially at the start of the season before hands have hardened, or on cold days, the coach should, if possible, use old and 'podgy' balls and be careful not to hit too hard. Even tennis-balls or other soft balls should not be ruled out for quite young boys, for the technique of judging and positioning can be learnt as well with them as with a match ball.

As an initial warming-up exercise he can divide his class into circles of six with an eight- to ten-yard radius, and for a few minutes make them throw quick under-hand catches to each other, whilst he walks round himself looking for such faults as unnecessary head movement, bad balance, and wrong positioning of the hands. Then he will get down to business.

For a 'full dress' fielding practice, six to eight boys are the ideal number, but of course, though it is uneconomic in time, a coach can deal with twice that number. They should be disposed in a half circle with their backs to any sun there is and the best available stretch of turf in front of them. A stump and a wicket-keeper, properly padded and gloved, complete the picture.

In the early practices of the season the coach should himself demonstrate the correct technique in catching and in both defensive and offensive fielding, emphasizing the essential points and giving the reasons for them. He will probably find it wise, especially in the earlier practices, to begin with defensive fielding, go on to offensive, and end by catching: by keeping these phases distinct, he will find that he can better emphasize the technique for each.

In hitting each ball the coach should call out the name of the fielder for whom it is intended: failure to do so will often mean indecision, frustration or even collision.

Each ball, whether fielded or caught, should be returned, whenever possible, full-pitch to the wicket-keeper, and the coach should hammer in that this, the final act of fielding, is just as vital as a stop or pick-up.

At the start each hit should be well within the compass of the fielders, but gradually their difficulty in pace, height or direction should be increased: e.g. low, fast catches, hit with 'cut', will be sent to potential covers, extra-covers or third-men, whilst, probably at the end of each session, the deep-fields will be catered for at range. This must be done both down and up wind, even sometimes 'down sun', and the importance driven home of not moving in to catches hit down wind until their flight has been fully judged. To practise quick sighting and judging of catches a coach may make his fielders stand with their backs to him and not look round until they hear the ball hit and their name called.

The close fields—the short legs, silly-mid-ons, and silly-points must be given special practice: for them far the best plan is for the coach to get someone to bowl to him from 12 yds or so away and play the ball at them as he might in a match. Here, of course, there will be no calling of names: it will be catch-as-catch-can.

The slip-fielders will practise at the slip-cradle if there is one, and may have a light curtain stretched 3 ft above the middle of the cradle to make it more difficult. With beginners it is most economical and effective if the coach or one fielder in rotation stands near the cradle and throws all the catches. The new plastic 'spring-board' also provides good practice.

The best slip-fielding practice is provided by one of the fielders in rotation throwing the ball fast from a range of from 8 to 10 yds, and full pitch so that the coach can slice it off the bat to slips and gully. This needs accurate throwing and considerable skill on the part of the coach, but it is far nearer the real thing than practice off the cradle and can stimulate the fielders into excited enjoyment and competition.

In a confined area excellent close catching practice can be given by the thrower standing behind two fielders facing a wall, and the latter having to sight and catch a solid rubber or tennis ball as it rebounds. This is of high value in quickening the fielders' reactions and can be made enjoyably competitive.

As soon as the coach is satisfied that his team has grasped the main principles of fielding technique, he will move on to the vital superstructure of 'match practice'.

It will be carried out in the middle; the coach will bat himself and, with someone bowling 'to order', will play strokes, as he would in a match, to a team stationed in their normal places, though, unless he and his bowler are pretty skilful, he may well dispense with slips and fine-leg.

Before he starts he will hammer home the following points:

(i) As the ball is bowled, all except the close fields should be just on the move towards the batsman with their weight balanced evenly and slightly forward. This movement will be accelerated to meet a slow moving ball, but checked if the ball is hit hard.

(ii) That every fielder, except first-slip and leg-slip, must be watching the bat and that intelligent vigilance will often succeed in anticipating the line of a stroke.

(iii) That they must stoop early and watch the ball into the hands before looking up.

(iv) That where possible returns should be full-pitch to the wicket-keeper and to effect this, the aim should be a foot or so above the stumps.

(v) That every throw-in must be properly backed up, and that, if he is to sight the ball properly and be able to cover a reasonable arc, the backer-up must be at least 10 yds away from the wicket.

(vi) That in chasing the ball, fielders must run at absolutely top pace and must overtake the ball before they stoop to pick it up.

(vii) That in a match every fielder must keep an eye on both captain and bowler all the time to catch an unobtrusive signal for an adjustment in their normal place. Once they are clear as to exactly where their captain and bowler want them to be, they must stick to that place and not wander about.

(viii) That it is criminal to make the bowler stoop: unless there is a chance of a run-out, the ball should be returned to him, if necessary by a relay system, a gentle catch at a comfortable height.

His sermon over, the coach will set to work as he might in a match, except that he will sometimes deliberately give chances and often call for what would be unjustifiably short runs. He may sometimes actually run the short single himself, for this can increase the fun. A 'come-two' or 'come-three', as he pierces the field should produce a desperate chase in reply. The fielders will, of course, 'let fly' whenever the call seems to offer a chance of a run-out, and for this reason it may be as well to have a second wicket-keeper doing duty at the bowler's end to save the latter's hands.

This match fielding practice can at times be most valuably combined with training batsmen in good running between the wickets.

Above all, the coach must throughout the practice encourage and commend: of course he must criticize when things are done wrongly, but when a good catch is made, there is a fine stop, or a fast and accurate return, let him make everyone feel that he is almost as delighted as the fielder himself: indeed he ought to be!

THE DEEP-FIELDS

With the decline of driving which has characterized most cricket in recent years, the importance, even the existence, of the true long-fields – long-on, long-off, and deep-mid-wicket has tended to diminish, though with the prevalence of short-of-a-length bowling directed at the leg stump and with the development of the hook, the role of deep-square and long-leg has gained in emphasis.

Of course no captain will weaken his attack by stationing men in the deep unless the batsmen force him to do so, but there are times when he will have no choice, especially when he is fighting to save runs against the clock, whilst nearly all slow leg-break bowlers and slow off-spinners, unless they are completely on top, will need one or more men deep on the on-side.

The chief qualifications for these deep-fields are:

(a) Pace to cut-off the fours or convert the possible twos into ones.

(b) Good hands for catching high and hard hits.

(c) A powerful and accurate throw.

To watch an expert deep-field sprint to intercept a hard drive, swoop down in his last few strides so that the ball runs into his hands, and then return it like an arrow full toss or first bounce to the wicket is to enjoy one of the glories of the game.

A deep-field may find the following considerations helpful:

(i) It is always easier to run in than to run back, so that he should err on the side of being too deep: but especially on big grounds he should not automatically think of his position as being 'on the boundary'. His distance from the batsmen will depend primarily on the estimated carrying distance of his full hit, and in his estimate the strength and direction of the wind must be given due weight.

(ii) He should always be moving in as the ball is bowled and watching first the ball and then the batsman: intelligence and experience will often enable him to anticipate the direction of the stroke and so get an invaluable start towards its interception.

(iii) On sighting a high hit in his direction, he should not immediately rush in but should wait until he has been able to judge the length and line of the ball accurately. Once he has done this, the sooner he can get into position for a catch and the more balanced and still he can be when it arrives, the better.

(iv) He should try to catch the ball chin-high, allowing his hands to give gently on impact.

(v) For length of return the over-hand, rather than the flat, throw is the best: for pace and carry a proper follow-through is essential.

(vi) A really fine thrower can sometimes run-out the striker at his end when going for a second run, especially if he is taking it easy in fancied security: it is possible to induce this sense of security by not at first moving in on the ball at full speed.

(vii) When an off-spin bowler is hit to the on, the ball tends to swing slightly to the fieldsman's right: this is the more true of all hits behind square-leg: they carry 'running side' and carry farther and arrive faster than at first seems likely.

MID-OFF

Whatever the bowler and whatever the state of the wicket, there will normally be a mid-off, though his actual position in the field may vary between wide limits. We are not concerned here with a true silly-mid-off except to suggest that this role can be easily overplayed and can lead – and has in fact frequently led – to a side virtually fielding with ten men. It is, of course, justifiable if the position is clearly unsettling and cramping a batsman, especially when he first comes in, or if he looks like playing the forward push to a left-hand spin or leg-break bowler which may lead to a catch close in. Only too often we see a silly-mid-off persistently retained on a good wicket when no prospect of such a catch is apparent and even after the initiative has clearly passed to the batsman.

For the normal mid-off the main qualifications are:

(i) Good strong hands to stop and, if need be, catch the hard hit.

(ii) Ability to start and move quickly to cut off the drive on either side of him, and to anticipate the stolen single from the push.

(iii) Courage, that will face up to anything that will come to him either on the ground or in the air, and that will get the legs and body behind the hands as a second line of defence.

(iv) An accurate, strong, low throw.

His position will be determined by:

(a) The pace of the ground.

(b) The bowler.

(c) The batsman.

(d) The position of the other off-side fielders: e.g. a short extra-cover will mean a deep-mid-off.

The faster the ground, the deeper can he stand to any batsman who is ready to off-drive, and still be able to save a single.

With an 'away swing', left-hand spin or leg-break bowler he will tend to stand appreciably wider than normal.

Mid-off will normally always aim at stopping the batsmen from running short singles; especially is this true when a man first comes in and is often on edge until he has 'broken his duck'.

By watching the batsman carefully he can often anticipate the probable line of the stroke.

For hard returns from the on-side it will often be mid-off's business to get to the wicket in order to save the bowler's hands.

There is no better place for a captain to field.

MID-ON

Fifty years ago mid-on was the place to which the weakest fielder in a team was generally assigned. Today in first-class cricket, with so much emphasis on the leg stump in attack and the development of on-side play, it is one of the most important.

Most of what has been written about mid-off is equally true of mid-on. His position too, both in depth and in angle to the batsman, will vary within wide limits, especially in relation to the nature of the bowler's attack and the placing of a forward square-leg: indeed none of the regular places is more elastic than mid-on. With the stock bowler attacking the off stump on a fast wicket, he may be about level with the bowler's wicket and some four yards to the right of it: conversely, with an off-spinner bowling round the wicket and really turning the ball, mid-on's normal position may be more or less covered by the combination of a forward square-leg and the bowler, and he may find himself 15 yds deeper and either almost behind the bowler or much wider in what is normally now known as 'mid-wicket'. As with mid-off he must always be prepared to save the bowler's hands by getting up to the wicket to take fast returns.

For him, as for mid-off, good hands, quickness of starting and a fast return are essential.

He should cultivate a fast under-hand 'flip' aimed at the bowler's wicket: particularly if he is standing deep, this may often provide a better chance of a run-out than a throw at the striker's wicket.

THE COVERS

Certainly on a fast wicket and to bowling directed at or outside the off stump the covers are the most spectacular places in the field and offer, perhaps, the greatest scope in run-saving. There is often, too, the chance of a catch from a spinning mishit or a fast-travelling slash.

Physical co-ordination, speed of foot, and accuracy and power of return are the chief qualifications for cover fielding.

The position of cover and extra-cover must be elastic, depending on the pace of the ground, the nature of the bowling and the batsman's normal stroke play.

On fast grounds they can afford to stand several yards deeper than on slow, and on these the ball tends to come 'squarer' from the bat: this is the more true for leg-spin and out-swerve bowling. On slow grounds and for off-spinners they will stand more in front of the wicket.

As a general principle they will start as deep as possible consistent with saving a single. A really fine cover-field can stand as much as 10 yds deeper than the ordinary performer and still save the single, whilst thus greatly increasing the arc within which he can cut-off the four, and incidentally tempting the batsman to risk a dangerous single.

More than any other fielders the covers will be on the move inward as the ball is bowled, watching the batsman and moving in with body balanced and inclined forward and with hands very much at the ready just in front of the thighs.

Directly the line of the ball from the stroke is clear, this movement will be accelerated into a swooping dash to intercept it at the earliest possible moment. In this dash the head and body will stoop so that at the moment of interception the head will be little more than 2 ft above the ground: the eyes will follow the ball right into the hands.

Speed and accuracy of return from the covers are essential both for run-outs and as a general deterrent of close-run singles. Though the 'over-hand' return is easier to direct accurately, nearly all the great covers use the 'flat' return at, or just below, the level of the shoulder.

In meeting and returning the short single, the under-hand wrist flick is often most effective.

Returns should, as a rule, be full-pitch to the wicket-keeper, i.e. a foot above the stumps. A direct throw at the stumps at the bowler's end is justifiable when there is a fair chance of a run-out: it is to be remembered that the batsman has farther to go and starts later than the backer-up: but this return needs much practice, for there is a natural tendency to 'pull' it: mid-on needs to be alert to back it up.

Some great covers have been able to camouflage this throw at the bowler's wicket by apparently aiming, until the last moment, at the wicket-keeper's end.

Experienced covers will not 'show their hand' unnecessarily: they may deliberately refrain from 'slipping into top gear' until there is a real chance of a kill.

A last caution: the squarer the hit in the cover direction, the more does the ball tend to curl from right to left.

THIRD-MAN

It is common to find a relatively weak fielder stationed at third-man, presumably on the ground that fewer catches go there than to any place in the field except deep-fine-leg. But on fast grounds and to off-side bowling

Peter Parfitt. The 'long barrier': the ball is being watched right into the hands

16a

Attack: head and body right down over the back foot and eyes glued to the ball.

The throw: the eyes are looking down the steering arm at the target and the throwing wrist is cocked

16b

'*For what we are about to receive*'

Tony Lock. A catch at slip: head and eyes right on the line and hands widely webbed

The England slips get down and stay down as Parfitt makes a fine diving catch

it is an important place, and if the batsmen are really good runners, only a fine fielder there can stop frequent singles or, if he is fielding deep to a fast bowler, prevent them running two.

Speed of foot and accuracy and pace of return are therefore the chief qualifications for this place.

The faster the ground and the bowling, the finer and deeper will third-man stand: but his angle to the wicket will also depend on the batsman's stroke play, i.e. finer, if he is a genuine cutter, or squarer, if he tends to play the short-of-a-length-ball with a forcing back-stroke.

If third-man is forced to drop back, the deeper he goes, the wider the arc he can cover, but he should always be able to save two to any ball which he can intercept.

The technique, if third-man is up, is roughly the same as for the covers: if he is back, it is the same as for the out-fields. But he must realize that the ball hit or edged to third-man always carries spin and tends to break away from right to left. He will therefore aim his point of interception well to the left of the initial line.

The bowler's end will as a rule supply the better chance of a run-out, but unless there really is such a chance, he must never bombard the bowler. Backing-up by third-man may be very important to wild returns from the on-side fielders.

THE CLOSE-IN FIELDS

In recent years the close-to-the-wicket places in the field have become increasingly specialized, and it is now generally accepted that they demand a technique of their own in the development of which experience plays a big part.

Of the qualifications necessary for them, physical co-ordination and quickness of reaction are the most important: big hands are another asset and so is reach, but this last must not be bought at the expense of speed.

For a quick reaction a **correct 'stance'** is essential (Fig. 5):

(i) The weight should be evenly distributed and balanced between both feet, placed comfortably apart but **not** straddled.

(ii) Both knees should be bent almost at right angles and the 'seat' must be well down if the fielder is to avoid unnecessary strain on the knees.

(iii) Some close-in fields start by resting their forearms on their knees, but before the ball is delivered the hands must come forward into the ready position: the balance of the body should now be on the balls of both feet and he should feel that he can instantly push forward or sideways off either foot. It is physically easier to rise than to stoop, and the lower the point of balance, the easier it is for the eyes of a close-in field to focus the majority of balls that come his way.

Fig. 5. The close field: body well down and balanced: fingers spread but not taut, head and eyes still and concentrated

(iv) Close-in fields tend to rise too early: a golden rule for them is **'get down and keep down and do not move until the ball has been really sighted off the bat'**.

(v) Above all, the head must be kept still so that the eyes can be truly focused and really watch the ball. Watch is perhaps too weak a word; **the fielder must concentrate to the extent of expecting and hoping that each ball will come to him.**

THE SHORT-LEGS

This section may well begin with a word of warning. The spectacle of a ring of 'leg-traps' is so common in first-class cricket today that it is often assumed to be a normal field disposition. This is an error, for in fact it can only be justified for a bowler who, whether by swing or by spin, is bringing the ball into the batsman: moreover it must assume a high degree of accuracy both in length and direction: without it the field is unbalanced, and the leg-traps must either be placed too far back to achieve their real purpose as wicket-takers or should, if the batsmen know their job, be liable to a risk of real physical injury to which young boys should never be exposed.

It is impossible to lay down any fixed rule as to the 'normal' position of a short-leg in depth or in angle to the batsman. The latter will depend on the pace of the wicket, the nature of the bowling, and, of course, on whether he is reinforced by other close-in fielders. But of depth it can be said at once that no boy should ever be stationed so near the wicket that he cannot sight the ball from a full-blooded hit. Given this reasonable margin of safety, a short-leg must never turn his back or retreat.

Short-leg, perhaps more than any other fielder, must be ready to chase the ball that is pushed past him. By quick starting, quick sprinting, and a fast and accurate return, the pick-up and throw being as nearly as possible one movement, he may often have the chance of a run-out; for batsmen are apt to misjudge short runs on the leg side. Similarly he may often prevent a second run and generally instil hesitation in the caller's mind.

He must always back up the wicket-keeper for returns from the covers: to do so effectively he must be at least 10 yds back from the wicket.

For backward short-leg and leg-slip the same general principles apply. These are more difficult places, for the ball comes 'round the corner' and it is almost impossible to anticipate the line.

They must remember that from off-spin bowlers the ball tends to move from the bat towards their right after hitting the ground.

Leg-slip to a fast bowler should be about a yard deeper than the wicket-keeper would be if standing back: he should watch the ball all the way and remember that the new ball tends to run off the edge of the bat more finely than the old.

THE SLIPS AND THE GULLY

These, with the close-leg fielders, are the most specialized of all positions, and in the training of them there is no substitute for experience.

The slip-cradle is valuable: some coaches become very skilful, with the help of an accurate bowler or thrower, in giving sliced catches off the face of the bat to fielders on the line of third-slip or wider: but only match experience can train a slip in the habit of concentration and give him something of what in the great slips seems to approximate to 'second sight'.

The qualifications, physical and mental, necessary for a slip are the same as for a close-in leg field.

The number and positioning of the slips must be elastic, according to the pace of the wicket and the bowling and the extent to which any bowler is, whether by spin or by swerve, moving the ball away from the bat.

For instance, on a plumb wicket a stock medium bowler who is not 'moving' the ball, may not be justified in having more than one slip and a gully, whereas on a crumbled wicket a slower bowler who is spinning the ball from leg may need two slips and a gully who will, of course, be stationed appreciably wider.

The depth of the slips will depend not only on the pace of the bowler and of the wicket, but even more on his lift off the pitch: the sharper the lift, the deeper they must be: the criterion must be the probable 'carry' of a snick off a good length ball. There is a general tendency for slips to stand too deep.

As regards their distance from each other, a word of caution is necessary against the popular 'yard-stick' of their being able just to touch each others fingertips at full arm stretch: if they can do so, they are too near and will be in danger of overlapping and interfering with each other's catches: there should be at least a foot between their outstretched hands.

First-slip must beware of standing too fine, especially when he is behind a wicket-keeper who tends to move right across to take the off-ball.

When there is no, or only a forward, short-leg, it will be first-slip's job to back-up throws from the off side, and to do this effectively he must not only get round to the leg side, but well back from the wicket-keeper.

The position of gully will depend on whether he expects to have to deal mainly with a sliced and edged stroke or with the genuine cut: if the batsman is a real cutter, he may well have to stand a yard or two deeper.

There is generally agreement that first-slip should watch the ball: whether second-slip should do so will depend on how fine he is standing: if he is at all wide, he should watch the outside edge of the bat: third-slip and gully will always do so.

Though it is generally true in all catching that two hands are safer than one, there are times, especially for the slips and gullies, when only a one-handed dive sideways or forward or both can hope to get to the ball in time to intercept it.

2

Wicket-Keeping

Of all positions in the field that of the wicket-keeper is at once the most important and the most exacting. Not only does he have more chances than any other fielder to intervene decisively in the game by catch, stump or run out, but he must be keyed up to anticipate such a chance with every ball of every innings. Moreover his form behind the stumps must have a profound effect on the morale not only of his bowlers but of the whole team: the feeling that they can rely on the skilful co-operation of their wicket-keeper will strongly reinforce the formers' confidence, whilst his keenness, vitality and general competence, especially in the taking of returns, can inspire and sustain his fellows through a long outing in the field.

It can therefore be laid down as an absolute principle in team selection that the best wicket-keeper, irrespective of all other considerations, should always be chosen.

The qualifications for the post are in the main the same as those necessary for any near-in fielder: quickness of eye and reaction, natural co-ordination, but to these must be added as especially desirable in his case, strong hands, physical courage and what can perhaps be described as mental, moral and physical stamina.

It is a common assumption that wicket-keepers are born and not made, but it is far from certain that all the best potential keepers naturally take to the gloves at an early age, and a coach would be wise at the start of the season to let any boy who has leanings in that direction try his hand, rather than run the risk of some potential Oldfield or Evans having been born to blush unseen. No long trial will be needed to determine whether a boy is or is not likely to become a wicket-keeper, but to become one in fact demands determination, training and prolonged practice.

Though there is no substitute for match experience in taking all sorts of bowling on all sorts of wickets, a good deal can be done for the young wicket-keeper in other ways. His first problem is to learn to take the ball properly, irrespective of any batsman in front of him: he can go a long way towards mastering this by getting someone to throw the ball at him, varying its length and direction, at a range of 10 to 15 yds, but he must play his part by concentrating, with every ball, on the correct use of the feet and hands and proper positioning and balance of the body as will be analysed later.

21

B 1697

This practice can be reinforced by the presence of a batsman, preferably with a cut-down bat, which will teach him to watch the ball in spite of the bat and to be on the look-out for chances of stumping. A word of caution should be said against making any young wicket-keeper 'keep' in an ordinary practice net: attention here is liable to be focused on the batsman and bowlers, the latter tend to bowl too soon after each other for his comfort, whilst the back net may make him feel constrained and even prevent him from standing back to a bowler whose pace demands it. Under no circumstances should he be made – or even allowed – to practise on a bad net wicket.

Equipment

For a wicket-keeper pads should be merely an incidental second line of defence, never to come into play unless by some mischance his first line – his hands – has been breached. This is equally true of taking returns as of taking the bowling: activity and accuracy in taking every throw, however wild, in the hands will in itself help to tidy up the fielding and will help the keeper to 'get and keep moving'. The special wicket-keeper's pads which are sometimes seen are an unnecessary emcumbrance: ordinary pads are perfectly adequate. He should always wear a 'protector': it will reinforce his confidence and may save him from serious injury.

He cannot take too much trouble over his gloves, for they are of vital importance to his art.

He should always wear a pair of 'inners', preferably of chamois leather, which should fit him **comfortably but not tightly,** for he may, if he gets bruised, want to reinforce them with padding or plasticine along the base of the fingers. Many wicket-keepers bind their fingers, or at least the fingers of their right hand, with surgical tape. The gloves proper must again fit comfortably but not tightly over the 'inners' and must be pulled right on so that the fingers fit well into the reinforced stalls.

New gloves tend to be stiff and unwieldy and must be battered pretty drastically into plasticity especially in the palm, the aim being to produce a cup effect.

Most wicket-keepers use some form of dressing on the face of their gloves to make them pliant and adhesive: the best is neat's foot oil which helps to make the gloves pliable and prevents them being slippery: on no account must they use any dressing which may make the ball 'tacky' to the detriment of the bowlers.

Position

A wicket-keeper must stand either right up or right back: there can be no half-way house. He should never hesitate to stand back to any bowling above medium pace or even to medium-paced bowling on very fast or 'lifting' pitches, if by so doing he will be improving his chance of taking the straight forward catch: for this is his first responsibility. No false pride, still less any instinct for showmanship, must weigh with him for a moment.

He can be encouraged too by remembering that most fast bowlers prefer to see their wicket-keeper standing back, and that by doing so he is much less likely to unsight first-slip and very much more likely to catch the leg snick.

How far back he will stand will obviously depend on the pace of the bowler and the nature of the pitch: the faster the bowler and the livelier the pitch, the farther back he will go. **But in general he will aim at so positioning himself that the good-length ball will reach him just after it starts to drop in its trajectory after pitching.**

Stance

The wicket-keeper's stance should ensure:
(i) **That he is comfortable and as little as possible conscious of any strain.**
(ii) **That he can get the best possible sight of the ball.**
(iii) **That he can take the ball with the minimum of movement.**
(iv) **That he is so close to the wicket that, after taking the ball, he can break it without having to reach for it at all.**

Most wicket-keepers today adopt the 'squatting' position, with the seat very close to the ground and the weight evenly distributed as well as balanced between both feet: the back of the hands will initially be resting on the ground between the legs (Fig. 1). The advantage of this position is

Fig. 1.
At rest: left foot behind middle and off stumps: body right down: gloves resting on ground with fingers downwards

that it minimizes muscular strain and provides the best possible sight of the ball.

The criterion of his stance is that it should enable him to get a perfect sight of the ball. To this end his left foot will be behind the middle and off stumps, the right will be parallel with it a comfortable distance away: each foot will be pointing directly down the pitch.

The body and head must be kept still, and it is of vital importance that they stay down as long as possible, only rising to meet the rise of the ball off the pitch. It is always easier to rise than to stoop.

The greatest wicket-keepers have always contrived to make their art look simple: with most of them indeed it has been so unobtrusive that spectators take if for granted.

This economy of movement is of the first importance for two reasons: it facilitates a true sighting of the ball, and it minimizes the fatigue of what is always an exacting and, in a long innings, can be an exhausting job.

The feet

The feet should move as little as possible but always enough to ensure that **the body is, as far as possible, behind the ball.** In taking balls to the off care must be taken to ensure that the right foot moves over parallel with, and never backwards away from, the crease (Fig. 2). If the right foot

Fig. 2.
A wider off ball:
note inward turn of
the right foot, to
lead balance back
towards the wicket

moves any real distance across, the left foot will naturally adjust itself accordingly.

The taking of balls to leg is the hardest part of the wicket-keeper's job, for not only has he to move farther over in order to get on to the line, but he has also to re-sight the ball after being at some stage in its course 'stymied' by the batsman's body. The instinct to move backward as well as across is even stronger on the leg side than on the off, but must be equally resisted. If the ball is at all wide, it will be necessary to move both feet (Figs. 3a and 3b).

If, in taking leg balls, the keeper will turn his left foot slightly inwards, he will find that it greatly helps his balance, i.e. his ability to leave his head behind, and to bring the ball once taken quickly back to the stumps. Ideally he should not move to take a leg ball until he has sighted it off the pitch.

The body

So far as possible the body should always be, or be brought on, to the line of the ball. There are two reasons for this: it will mean that the head and eyes are thus positioned to sight the ball, and if the hands fail to take it

Fig. 3a.
Taking a leg ball:
notice the slight inward
turn of the left foot

it will be intercepted by the body and a catch may even be made on the rebound from it (Fig. 4).

The hands

There are two vital principles to which the hands must conform.

 (i) **Unless the ball is so wide or so high as to make it impossible, they should always take it with the fingers pointing down: they should never be pointed at the ball.** They must not be rigid, but held in a relaxed cup, with the feeling that they are padded cushions into which the ball will sink and naturally remain.

(ii) **They must 'ride' with the ball,** that is to say, carry back several inches as it enters them: this minimizes the tendency for the ball to jump out as well as the risk of bruising.

The young wicket-keeper must try to cultivate the habit of bringing the ball back to the wicket directly this 'ride' is over and the ball is secure: he should even go through the motion, though the batsman has played the ball.

Concentration

So far we have been concerned with the pure mechanics of wicket-keeping, but they will be of no avail unless they are reinforced by **the most relentless concentration and the most vigilant watching of the ball.** This must become an instinctive habit, but will only do so if he constantly strives for it.

The wicket-keeper **must** assume that **every** ball will reach him, even the

Fig. 3b.
A wider and rising ball to leg: the right foot has followed the left; the hands and body are 'riding' with the ball

Fig. 4.
Taking the length ball just
outside the off stump: the
right foot has moved across
to bring the head on to the
line: notice the position of
the hands

most comfortable full-pitch which it would seem impossible for the batsman to miss.

Like the batsman, he must watch the bowler's hand and watch the ball
not only in the air but off the pitch. To do this effectively and to go on
doing it, he must banish everything else from his mind. He must never be
upset by setbacks, nor must he be deluded by success into thinking his job
easy: it never is. Of course he will miss more catches than other fielders, for
he will get more: what matters is the proportion of reasonable chances
that he accepts.

Stumping

In the vast majority of cases where a chance of stumping is missed the
failure is due to one or other of three very natural temptations:

(i) Looking at the bat and assuming that the ball will hit it.

(ii) Looking up before the ball is taken.

(iii) Snatching at the ball.

The young wicket-keeper must try to keep his mind free from any 'stumping preoccupation' which may all too easily lead to the two last faults just mentioned: **if only he takes the ball right, the breaking of the wicket will follow naturally.**

It is impossible to watch the ball and the batsman at the same time: it is the ball that matters.

Experience will create an instinct for the type of ball and the type of stroke that may provide a chance of stumping: sometimes the keeper will break the wicket only to find that the batsman has never left his ground: that is all in the game, but he must try not to appeal!

Taking returns from the field

Accuracy and agility by the wicket-keeper in taking the returns from his field are not only essential for effecting run-outs, but are of high importance in sustaining general morale and in deterring batsmen from taking short runs.

He must always position himself directly behind and very close to the stumps, facing directly down the line of the return: to do this, if he is standing back, will mean a very quick start from his original position.

The technique for taking the ball will be the same as if it came from the bowler.

However inaccurate the throw-in, he must try to take it cleanly in his hands and never be content to stop it with his pads.

In taking wide returns he must move across to the line, so positioning himself as to bring the ball back to the stumps; the wider the return the more must his outside foot point inwards, thus facilitating the forward balance towards the stumps. In taking returns which reach him on the half volley, he must get right behind the line, with feet close together, get down and stay down.

As in stumping, so in run-outs, he must concentrate on the ball and never look at the running batsman.

Whilst shunning any form of showmanship, a wicket-keeper must by his activity and general liveliness make himself felt behind the wicket as a focus to the fielding side.

He should expect and encourage his fielders to throw in fast and accurately to him, even when no run is attempted. It will keep him warm and agile, it will give them the range, and it will make the batsman think.

If a catch is skied near the wicket and his captain does not, as he should, call him by name, the wicket-keeper must not hesitate to shout 'Mine' loudly and clearly and go for the catch: once he does so, he should go on with it at all costs.

He must learn to throw the ball accurately to the bowler or, on the relay system, to a suitable fielder. It is criminal to make the bowler stoop.

If at any time his hands become really bruised, he should take a rest from wicket-keeping at once rather than try to hang on and risk being out of the game for much longer.

Finally, a wicket-keeper must keep really fit: unless he does so, he cannot hope to command through a long day in the field the vigilant concentration and sustained activity which his job demands and which will mean so much to his side.

3

Bowling

No matter how many runs a cricket team make, they cannot win a match until they have dismissed their opponents. The latter may, of course, assist the process by varieties of cricket suicide, but in the main it is the bowler who has to get them out. The better the class of cricket and the better the pitch, the more true it is that, **whilst the batsman saves matches, it is the bowler who wins them.** In Test Match cricket the rubber has been determined far more often by superiority in bowling than in batting.

Bowling is not a natural technique, any more than batting: it has to be learnt and practised: but whereas both demand a certain degree of physical co-ordination, the bowler need not be born with the quickness of eye and reaction that are necessary for real batting skill. **Given a reasonable start by sound instruction, the opportunity to practise, some intelligence, but above all real determination and enthusiasm, most boys can become good enough to enjoy bowling and to be of value as bowlers to their side.**

Every boy will eventually make up his own mind how he wants to bowl, but a coach can help to guide his choice wisely. In the sections that follow, some suggestions are made as to the physical and 'mental' qualifications that make for success in different types of bowling. But whichever type a boy decides to adopt, a coach must try to impress on him that bowling is not just mechanical but, even for a fast bowler, a craft and an art demanding real study and application; above all, that it can only be mastered by practice. There is no easy way.

The aim of the bowler, whether he is fast, medium or slow, is to defeat the batsman opposed to him: it may be by the direct assault of pace, by the deception of spin and flight, by sheer persistency or by a combination of all three. But to do this economically **he must be able to command accuracy in length and direction.** This accuracy is the very foundation of his craft, and to establish it he will need a determined mind and a good action.

The importance of concentration for a batsman is constantly stressed: it is no less true for the bowler. It can only be acquired by will-power and practice.

As he starts his run up for each ball the bowler should have a clear mental picture of what he wants and means to bowl: the more he can convince himself that he can, and is going to, bowl the ball he wants, the more likely he is to bowl it: confidence is a great asset in bowling and can be built up in practice.

The bowler must constantly remind himself that the initiative lies with him, and that he must do everything he can to retain it. Whatever his method of attack, it must be inspired and sustained by a proper hostility to the batsman.

By encouragement and suggestion the coach can do much to reinforce a bowler's resolution and to increase his resource, but the greatest service he can do him will be to help him bowl with a good action.

THE BASIC ACTION

Bowling actions vary in practice as greatly as batting styles, but in both there are certain fundamentals which are essential to success. Though some good bowlers, and even a few great bowlers, may seem to violate some of these fundamentals, they are good in spite, not because, of such violations, which indeed are generally more apparent than real.

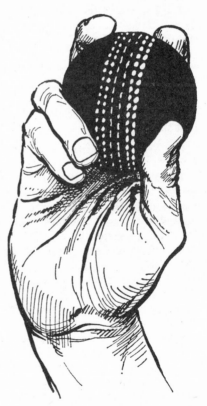

As will be indicated in the separate section allotted to him, the genuine leg-spin bowler may need to make some adjustment in the principles set out below. But for all other types these principles hold good, and only by adhering to them can bowlers hope to make the most of their natural gifts.

The fundamentals of a good bowling action are:

(i) **A correct grip.**
(ii) **A smooth and economical run-up.**
(iii) **An easy, rhythmical and well-balanced delivery, making full use of your height and body.**
(iv) **A deliberate and fluent follow-through.**

The grip

The grip of the ball will, of course, vary according to the type of ball which the bowler intends to deliver: such varieties in grip will be discussed later. **But for all types of bowling it is**

Fig. 1. A basic grip

essential that the ball should be held in the fingers and not in the palm of the hand. Only so can the bowler have full control of the ball and the fingers, as the final extension of the wrist imparts that whip which will give the ball life off the pitch.

The run-up

The object of the run-up is to bring the bowler to the bowling crease completely balanced and with the momentum necessary to bowl, and keep on bowling, at his normal, designed pace. Its length should be the minimum necessary to provide this momentum. It should be smooth and regular without hops or changes of step.

The run should 'build up': in other words, the bowler should start slowly, even walking the first pace or two, and then gradually increase his speed: it is only in the last few strides that the full momentum should be reached.

The balance of the body should be slightly forward and carried on the front of the feet. The muscles should be relaxed but there should be throughout a feeling of 'tidiness' and control. The head should be kept as still as possible.

As has already been said, the bowler should have a clear idea before he starts his run-up what he intends to bowl: during the run-up he should watch the batsman closely until he has finally made up his mind where he means to pitch the ball: he should then fix his eyes and his mind on that spot.

The delivery

There are five key positions through which a bowler should pass in his delivery. In broad principle, the first two represent the winding up of the body and the last two its unwinding into the actual bowling of the ball and the follow-through. The third position, the half-way stage between the two phases of the action, is one with which nearly all the great bowlers have in fact conformed. Each and all of these positions are integral to the action. One bowler, for instance, may conform to the principles of Positions 1, 2 and 3 but not that of Position 5 and fail to follow through. Another, though following through well, may violate one or more of the principles of Positions 1, 2 and 3, and either not pivot correctly or bowl 'full-chested'. It is the bowler's ability to co-ordinate the correct movements of the body, arms and feet at each position or stage of his action that gives rhythm and 'timing' to the delivery: without these he will certainly lack life off the pitch and accuracy in length and direction.

The action now to be analysed is that of a right-hand bowler of medium pace; but the general principles will be found to hold good for all types of bowling.

Maurice Tate. 'The spring is cocked': weight well back and body sideways; head perfectly poised

32a

Ray Lindwall. A fine study of a fast bowler's approach to the crease: the high right arm makes for a long delivery swing

Harold Larwood. Poise, power and pace

Fred Truman. Though the weight has almost reached the front foot, the left shoulder is still pointing at the batsman, with the head looking down the wicket, behind a high front arm

32d

The Basic Action: position 1   *The Basic Action: position 2*

POSITION 1

The last stride of the run-up prior to the 'delivery stride' is more or less
a jump off the left foot. To assist this movement the left foot will turn
inward and the left arm begin to swing upward in the last but one stride.
This turning movement from the run-up into delivery is a vital condition of
the whole bowling action. Position 1 represents the moment in this stride
when the right foot and body have started to turn sideways; the right hand
is close to the face, and the left arm is stretching upwards. This is, in fact,
the start of the winding-up of the body.

POSITION 2

The right foot has landed just behind and parallel to the crease; the body
has completed a half-turn so that the left shoulder is pointing at the batsman;
the left arm, though not rigid, is extended upwards, and the bowler is looking

up the pitch from behind it; the weight is on the right foot, and the body is leaning slightly away from the batsman; the back is slightly arched; the right arm has started on the delivery swing.

There is good reason behind all this. The placing of the right foot parallel to the crease ensures a good sideways turn of the body: the left shoulder pointing towards the batsman and the arching of the back will produce the maximum pivot: the high left arm is ready to lead the pivot, and the weight now leaning away from the batsman will add to the momentum as the body swings forward on to the left foot and the ball is delivered.

Position 2 is of the utmost importance, since it represents the completion of the winding-up of the body; errors at this stage of the action cannot be compensated later. The spring is now cocked and ready for release.

The 'delivery stride' now takes shape. While the body swings forward, led by the left shoulder, hip and leg, the left arm is thrown out towards the batsman and the right arm comes up with the wrist slightly delayed or 'cocked'; this movement of the arms is rather like a cartwheel.

The left foot lands flat directly in line with the right and pointing towards long-leg: it should never land on the off side (i.e. to the left) of that line; though to land appreciably to the on side of it is undesirable, some small deviation in this direction is possible without interfering with the follow-through. The length of the 'delivery stride' must depend upon the bowler's physique: its function is to provide a firm and adequate axis for the delivery. Too short a stride will prevent the bowler from making full use of his body: too long a stride will result in loss of height and balance at the moment of delivery.

The object of placing the left foot in line with the right, and pointing not straighter than towards long-leg at the beginning of the delivery stride, is to help to keep the left shoulder and hip pointing at the batsman for as long as possible. The shoulders start to turn and are followed by the hips just, and only just, before the weight reaches the front, or left, foot. If the unwinding of the body begins at an earlier stage the bowler will inevitably deliver the ball 'full-chested', and thus mainly with his arm. This means that he will have failed to make full use of his body at the critical moment and will have destroyed the rhythm and timing of his action upon which life and accuracy so largely depend.

Throughout the delivery stride, and indeed throughout the whole action, the head must be kept as still as possible.

POSITION 3

This is the half-way stage: the weight is on the point of being transferred from the back foot to the front; the right arm is half-way up its delivery swing; the left shoulder is still pointing down the wicket and the head is looking at the target along the extended left arm which is 'striking' at it.

The Basic Action: position 3

A vital phase, if full use of the body is to be made in the delivery: on no account must the left shoulder be allowed to fall away towards gulley.

POSITION 4

This is the moment when the ball is delivered. The full weight of the body is now firmly on the left leg, and the left side is as braced as possible: the shoulders and hips have completed a half-turn: the right arm is straight and high above the head and the wrist has 'uncocked'.

The braced left side 'gives something to bowl against' and together with the high right arm ensures that the bowler is making full use of his height. The cocking and uncocking of the wrist add 'whip' to the delivery: this in no sense constitutes a 'throw'.

POSITION 5

This is the start of the follow-through. The pivot has now been completed and the right shoulder is nearly pointing at the batsman. The body has swung right through, and the weight has passed beyond the left leg. The right leg is in the process of being carried over and past the left: this means that the leg must to some extent be flexed at the knee, otherwise it will tend to swing wide and 'square' the body too soon. The head must not drop sideways and the eyes should still be looking up the pitch. The left arm having passed close to the

The Basic Action: position 4   *The Basic Action: position 5*

body has swung well back and beyond it, and the right arm has followed it over to the left thigh. The left arm has thus completed more than a half circle, and the right arm has swung down from the level of the face, up again above the head and down to the left thigh.

But the action is still not completed. The follow-through must be continued for several paces. If it is not, the action will be stunted and 'jerky', and the rhythm lost. In these final strides the bowler should not turn off too sharply to the off side but at the same time he must be careful not to run on the pitch, as this is a fault which is often difficult to correct later on.

The most common faults in bowling (right-arm bowlers) are:
(i) Not making a consistent and gradually accelerating run up to the wicket.
(ii) Not landing with the back foot parallel with the bowling crease in the delivery stride.

(iii) Not getting the right arm high enough in the delivery.
(iv) Not looking down the wicket from behind the left shoulder.
(v) Allowing the left shoulder to open too early and so bowling too full chested.
(vi) Allowing the front leg to crumple and so losing height in delivery.
(vii) Not following right through.
(viii) Not concentrating the eyes and the mind on the exact spot where each ball is meant to drop.

SWERVE

'Swerve' is dealt with thus early in the bowling section, not because it is rated of higher importance than spin, but because, given certain conditions, almost every fast, medium, or even slow bowler, whose action conforms in the main to the principles analysed on pp. 31–37, can make the ball swerve. Sometimes, indeed, they will find that they cannot stop it from swerving. **But the coach must impress on his bowlers that the mere ability to make the ball 'move in the air' is of little value unless it is combined with accuracy, accuracy of length of course, but in this case above all of direction.** Very few bowlers are justified in regarding swerve as their sole stock-in-trade: they must have other resources on which to draw.

There is no need to enter into the various scientific explanations as to why a cricket ball swerves: but certain conditions undoubtedly favour it:
(i) A heavy atmosphere.
(ii) A wind from the right quarter.
(iii) A new or relatively new ball, or at least a ball with a still prominent seam.

The bowler can do much to keep the seam clean, but the fielders must co-operate by trying to keep the shine on the ball for as long as possible.

On what is now commonly called a 'green' wicket, i.e. one on which there is a lot of grass still retaining moisture, the normal mechanics for the swerve sometimes make the ball 'move' when it hits the ground.

OUT-SWERVE

In recent years the cult of the in-swerve has been so great, and boys who watch first-class cricket are so accustomed to seeing this type of bowling, supported by a leg-side field, that they are apt to take it as their model. It is also true that the in-swerve is easier to bowl than the out-swerve, for the latter demands a full body pivot and a good follow-through as described in the analysis of the action below, whilst the in-swerve can be – and often is – bowled full-chested. **But nearly all great batsmen are agreed that it is the ball which 'runs away from them' late in its flight which is the most**

dangerous, and the bowler who can command it, even if only in his opening overs, may well strike a vital blow for his side.

The grip

Every bowler must work out for himself the grip which suits his action best. But in the main he is likely to find that it will conform with the following:

(i) The seam is 'canted' slightly in the direction of the intended swerve, i.e. towards first slip.

(ii) The first and second fingers will be on top of the ball roughly on each side of the seam. With the ball thus canted, however, they must obviously lie slightly across it, the right side of the thumb will lie directly beneath it (Fig. 2a).

Though the 'canting' of the seam undoubtedly promotes swerve, it may also tend to start it early in the ball's flight. The later the swerve, the more dangerous it is, and some of the best 'late-swervers' urge that the seam should not be 'canted' but kept vertical: they maintain that, provided the bowler's action is right, the ball will still swerve but later in its flight. In any event it is probable that bowlers will find it necessary to experiment from time to time with minor adjustments in the angle of the seam.

The action

For out-swerve the normal shoulder pivot should be slightly exaggerated, i.e. the batsman should see rather more of the bowler's left shoulder just before the body starts to unwind; in the follow-through, which should be more pronounced, the right hand should swing down and across to finish close to the left thigh. The wrist should perhaps be kept a little stiffer than for the normal delivery and the bowler should feel, as his arm comes over, that his first two fingers are kept fully behind the ball for as long as possible, in fact until the moment of release. This is very important and to assist it the angle of the wrist should remain constant well into the follow-through.

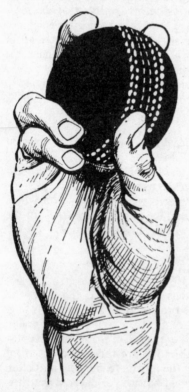

Fig. 2a. Grip for the out-swerve

Though it is true that to drop the level of the arm in the delivery swing may increase the out-swerve, the ball so delivered will as a rule start to swerve earlier in its flight. The later the swerve, the more dangerous it is, and **it is the high action delivery that makes the ball swerve late.**

It is easier to bowl the out-swerve from close up against the wicket, but if the bowler can make the ball swerve from a little wider on the crease, it is a more difficult ball because of its angle of approach to the batsman and the fact that it will tend to swing later.

Use of the out-swerve

The coach should insist that, to be effective, the bowler must bowl straight or at least straight enough to make the batsman play at the ball, and if possible to make him play forward to it. There are two reasons for this; firstly, it provides much less of a problem to the batsman if he is given plenty of time to watch and play it off the back foot; secondly, the farther up the ball is pitched, the more 'room' it has in which to swing. **To waste the new ball by bowling 'swingers' outside the off stump at which the batsman need not play is a bowling crime;** it takes the shine off the ball, tires the bowler to no purpose and gives the batsman a free sight of the swerve. The swerve must not be used automatically, or the batsman will soon become 'acclimatized' and adjust his strokes to it. It should be varied with an occasional straight ball, possibly bowled with the fingers across and not down the seam.

Bowlers will sometimes find that the ball, though meant to swerve out, unexpectedly comes in off the pitch: this has never been adequately accounted for, but either of the following reasons may be valid: it may be due to the seam hitting the ground at a different angle, or what is known as 'action-break', i.e. spin imparted by the full pivot of the body; or again to 'cut'. This can sometimes be produced deliberately by the bowler delivering the ball with the normal action for the out-swerve but with a slightly more arched back and with the seam 'canted' inwards as for the in-swinger (see below).

IN-SWERVE

It is easier to make the ball swerve in, but difficult to do so with consistent control of length and direction. The inaccurate in-swinger is a terrible problem for his captain, for he is bound to be expensive and may well be a real menace to the close fielders on the leg-side. But bowled accurately and supported by good catching, the in-swinger can be very effective against all but the most experienced batsman.

The grip

As with out-swerve, bowlers must experiment for themselves, especially with the angle of the seam, but the normal grip will be as follows:

(i) The seam of the ball will be 'canted' slightly to fine leg.

(ii) The first and second fingers will lie on top of the ball roughly parallel with the seam, with the second finger running along the inner or 'off' side of it: the ball of the thumb will be more or less directly beneath them (Fig. 2b).

The action

Little change in the basic action is necessary: **in the 'delivery stride' the left foot should land slightly to the off side of the right instead of in line with it: the arch in the back should be somewhat accentuated: the right arm should come over as close to the head as possible and, instead of swinging across the body, should come down in front of it and finish past the right thigh.** The left shoulder will thus tend to swing away earlier and the body at the moment of delivery to be more 'full-chested' to the batsman. These adjustments make it easier for **the hand to 'cut down' on the near side of the ball**: this is essential to the bowling of the in-swerve. It is, of course, easier to swing the ball in from the off if it is delivered from wide on the crease rather than from close to the wicket, but this presents less of a problem to the batsman because of its angle of approach to him.

Use of the in-swerve

The bowler must normally bowl to hit the wicket and aim to bring the batsman pushing forward on the front leg. Many batsmen, when playing forward, tend to leave a gap between bat and pad, commonly called 'leaving the gate open', in which case the well-pitched-up ball that moves late from the off may well slip through. Alternatively, since he is forced to play at the ball, he may well edge a catch to one of the close-leg fieldsmen. A yorker, swinging in on to the leg stump, is always a dangerous ball. The bowler must never forget that whereas a batsman may easily get himself out to the ball that swerves away wide of the off stump, he is much less likely to do so to the ball that swerves in

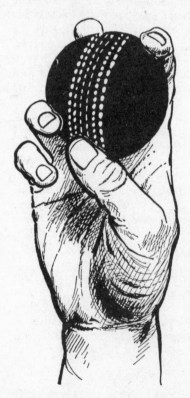

Fig. 2b. Grip for the in-swerve

Alec Bedser: a perfect follow-through

C. V. Grimmett. Leg-spin: a full body-pivot has reinforced the fingers and wrist

Jim Laker just after delivery in the Test Match in which he took 19 wickets

40b

to pass outside his legs: a mishit off it is more likely to produce runs than a wicket, whilst, if it is missed, the wicket-keeper is set a problem. Control of direction is of the first importance.

The leg-cutter

The term leg-cutter is used to describe a technique closely allied to that of the in-swinger, but one through which, by cutting or pulling the finger across the seam of the ball at the moment of delivery, leg-spin is imparted to it. The ball is held between the first and second fingers with the second finger pressing firmly on the inside edge of the seam and the first finger comfortably spaced from it on the smooth surface (Fig. 3). The thumb is underneath and on the side of the seam. At the moment of delivery the second finger pulls on the seam, the thumb pushes and the wrist rotates outwards, thus causing the ball to spin from the leg. The arm must be kept high in the delivery and there must be a full and vigorous follow-through.

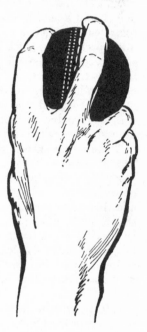

Fig. 3. Leg-cutter

To be effective, the leg-cutter must be bowled to a full length thus forcing the batsman to play forward. The line of attack will be the middle and leg stumps and, in as much as the grip and the delivery is closely allied to that of the in-swinger, some balls meant to be leg-cutters will in fact go straight on, or even move into the batsman. It is therefore desirable to have two short legs, one just in front of and the other behind the wicket and close enough to catch the edged or half-edged ball. If the bowler is accurate and the leg-cutter is really biting, he may justifiably have two gullies, one of whom will be almost as square as the old fashioned point.

This section must end with a final word of caution. As has been said, it is not difficult, given favourable conditions, to bowl both the out- and the in-swerve: but to do so successfully, real control of direction is essential, i.e. the bowler with a field set for a normal out-swerve must, if he bowls an in-swerve, start it on a line on or just outside the off stump, and conversely, his colleague, bowling to an in-swerve field, must, if he tries an out-swerve, aim it at the middle or middle-and-leg. **The young bowler had much better concentrate on one type of swerve or the other, set his field accordingly, and make only very occasional use of the other swerve.**

FAST BOWLING

It is probably true to say that at the start of their cricket lives most small boys want to bowl as fast as they can: it is a natural way of 'letting off steam', it is exhilarating to see the bails fly, and on the pitches upon which many of them play even moderate pace is likely to be formidable to young batsmen and to reap a fair crop of wickets.

But as he moves into a higher class of cricket and on to the better pitches that should attend it, the young bowler will find it a different story. **To a competent batsman on a good wicket nothing is more welcome than a bowler whose pace may be quick but is not really fast and who is inaccurate in length and direction.** If a boy is to have a real future as a fast bowler, the coach must try to ensure that the foundations are there and have not been undermined by his trying to bowl too fast for his age and strength. Fast bowling demands as initial qualifications strength of legs, back and rump, together with stamina and a certain aggressiveness of temper. But these will achieve little unless they operate through a good action.

On no account must a young fast bowler be allowed to 'over bowl' either in pace or duration: he must try to be patient and wait for his pace to develop gradually as his strength and stamina increase: at every stage his standard pace should be such as he can hope to sustain for several overs at a stretch and then to reproduce in later spells. Neither in a match nor in practice should he be allowed to bowl for long at a time; in a match he should be used in short spells, and be taken off before he shows any signs of tiring, so that he can 'come again'. At a net he may 'warm up' gradually to his full pace but he should have already done this before he takes the field to bowl his opening over in a match, especially if the weather is cold.

A fast bowler must be particularly careful to look after his feet: he cannot bowl properly if they are blistered or bruised: thick socks are essential and many bowlers like to wear two pairs. **He must, of course, see that he is properly nailed and that the nails are clear of dirt.**

The action

The principles laid down for the Basic Action (pp. 31–37) are particularly vital for fast bowlers, as real pace demands perfect rhythm and timing and these in turn depend on the right harnessing of every part of the body throughout the action. The coach must do everything possible to help the boy to understand these principles and the importance of trying to bowl according to them.

A good run-up is essential. In trying for pace many boy bowlers 'charge' up to the wicket instead of building up the approach by gradual acceleration. Many run too far. A properly timed acceleration over a dozen or so paces will provide a much greater final momentum than a longer 'sprint' in which there is very likely a check or a stammer before reaching the crease. Larwood's and Lindwall's deliveries always appeared to be the natural and inevitable climax of a perfectly controlled and rhythmic approach.

The jump which in some degree all bowlers make before landing in Position 2 of the Basic Action may well, in the case of fast bowlers, be slightly accentuated. The delivery swing of the right arm must be long and complete. The follow-through should be pronounced, taking him several paces beyond the crease and of course well clear of the pitch; for this reason, if for no other, a fast bowler should bowl 'over the wicket'.

Tactics

(*Note:* the following applies only to bowlers whose pace, relative to the batsmen opposed to them, is unmistakably fast. If it is only 'fastish', the tactics suggested for the medium-paced bowler are more relevant.)

The role of the fast bowler is essentially to attack and he need not concern himself with any other. He is generally given the new ball and therefore should study carefully the art of 'swerve'. If his action is really good, he will probably be able to make a new ball swing away and sometimes to bring it back from the off after pitching. But pace must always be his main weapon.

He must bowl straight enough to make the batsman play: for this reason he should always have a deep-fine-leg, for without it he may not have the confidence to do so, since a snick on the leg side would then always mean 'Four'.

The greater his pace and the faster the wicket, the greater is the bowler's margin of length, and fast bowlers can, and indeed should, vary their length more than others. Every new batsman should be tested very early in his innings by a 'yorker'; but a true yorker is a difficult ball to bowl, and a really 'full' half-volley, provided it is fast enough, has a very good chance of getting through. Alternatively, at the start of his innings an extra fast ball bowled just short of a length may find the batsman fatally late on his back-stroke.

Then there is the genuinely short ball into which the bowler 'puts everything that he has got' in the hope that it may lift to an uncomfortable height. Provided that it is only bowled occasionally, and is not aimed at the batsman, it is a perfectly legitimate test of his morale and technique. A timid batsman is likely to flinch from it and edge it; a braver player will almost certainly try to hook it and may easily mistime it and get caught; but to be effective, this type of ball must be really fast and so must the wicket. If called upon to bowl on a dead wicket, the bowler must virtually cut out the short ball and try to make the batsman play forward: if he is accurate enough, he may under these conditions bring one or even two fielders close in in front of the wicket.

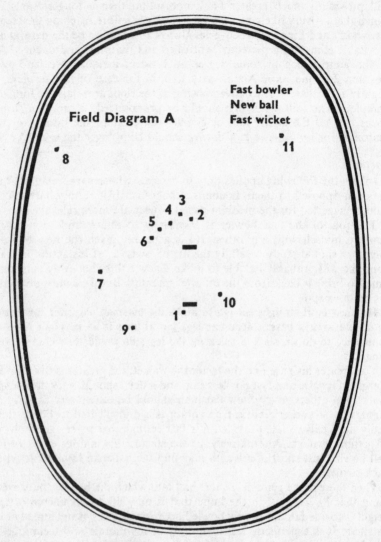

Field Diagram A

**Fast bowler
New ball
Fast wicket**

1. Bowler	4. Second-slip	7. Cover-point	10. Forward-short-leg
2. Wicket-keeper	5. Third-slip	8. Third-man	11. Deep-fine-leg
3. First-slip	6. Gully	9. Mid-off	

If the bowler is making the ball swing away, mid-off will be rather wider, cover-point will be almost square and as deep as possible provided that he can 'save' one. If the bowler is moving the ball in, rather than out, third-slip will be brought over to leg-slip, third-man will be square and cover more in front of the wicket.

Again, when the wicket is really helping him, he must eschew experiment, bowl straight and keep the ball up: by doing so he will give it more 'room to do things' in the air; it is bound to 'do things' off the ground. The exact positioning of his slips and gully is most important. The faster and livelier the pitch, the deeper they must be: their criterion must be the probable 'carry' of a snick off a good length ball. Slips also tend to stand too close to each other.

Some last reflections suggest themselves. **Fast bowling demands a high degree of general, and particularly muscular, fitness,** and to attain it the bowler must be prepared to discipline himself and work hard. **He must be master of himself whether things are going well or ill.** If the tide is running with him, he must be on his guard against getting excited for, if he does, he may well start rushing up to the wicket, lose his rhythm and bowl 'all over the place'. If, on the other hand, things go against him, he must equally keep his head and at the same time harden his heart. **It is probably more true of a fast bowler than of any other that in the long run the man who never gives up trying will have most success.**

MEDIUM-PACE BOWLING

In all classes of cricket medium-paced bowlers predominate. Moreover, they are a *sine qua non* in any side, as they can be used on any wicket. They can be deadly under favourable conditions and, when the wicket is plumb or when the batting side is chasing runs against the clock, invaluable in pinning the batsmen down by bowling to a properly placed field with real determination and control of length and direction. **If pace and fire are the great virtues for a fast bowler, and spin and cunning for a slow, it is for this accuracy that the medium-paced bowler is asked above everything.**

On a wicket of normal pace his margin of accuracy may be roughly defined as some 4 to 5 ft in length and in direction to the area between the middle stump and a few inches outside the off stump.

If the bowler is to achieve this general control, the coach must try to ensure that the mechanics of his action are right, i.e. that they conform in the main to the principles laid down in the section on the Basic Action (see pp. 31–37). Then he must convince him that only by constant, intelligent and resolute practice can he hope to get very far: **the bowler must, in fact, condition not only his body but his mind until the first has the control, and the second has the will and the confidence, to bowl a length and to bowl it in the right direction.** But uniform and mechanical accuracy of length and direction, though it may be effective enough on bad wickets or against unskilful batsmen, will not prove formidable against good batsmen on good wickets. A medium-paced bowler must set his standards higher than this: he must try to attain control of variations in length within the general limits already set down and to be able to camouflage those variations and

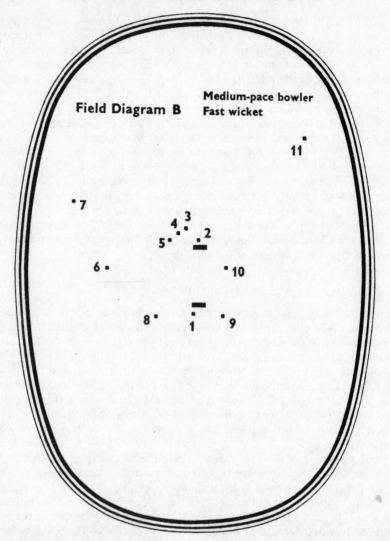

Field Diagram B   **Medium-pace bowler**
Fast wicket

1. Bowler   4. Second-slip   7. Third-man   10. Forward-short-leg
2. Wicket-keeper   5. Gully   8. Mid-off   11. Deep-fine-leg
3. First-slip   6. Cover-point   9. Mid-on

If opposed to a strong off-driver, he may be forced to have a deep extra-cover instead of a forward-short-leg: in that case mid-off will be rather wider and closer to save the short single: alternatively he may keep an extra-cover up to 'save one' and drop mid-off well back and relatively straight.

When the shine is off the ball, and particularly if he finds that he can bring it back appreciably from the off, he should bring second-slip over to short-leg behind the wicket.

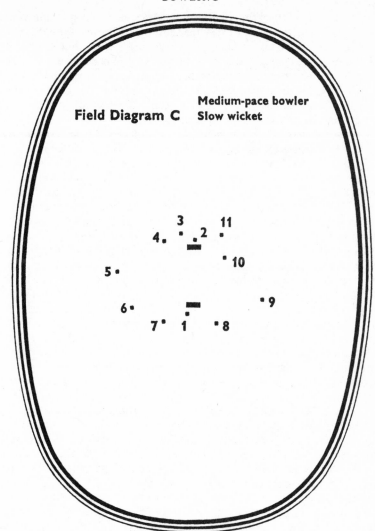

Field Diagram C **Medium-pace bowler Slow wicket**

1. Bowler
2. Wicket-keeper
3. First-slip
4. Short-third-man
5. Cover-point
6. Extra-cover
7. Mid-off
8. Mid-on
9. Mid-wicket
10. Forward-short-leg
11. Backward-short-leg

If the bowler finds himself being attacked off the front foot, he may have to drop mid-off and mid-on back deeper and in necessity, even drop mid-wicket back to the boundary.

If the ball is turning sharply and the bowler is being driven 'with the break', he will have to move his long-on wider and perhaps dispense with his extra-cover, moving him into the deep field almost straight behind him.

to reinforce them with spin and swerve. The mechanics of spin and swerve are dealt with elsewhere, and every medium-paced bowler should hope to be able to make some use of them. But he should not attempt to bowl leg-breaks; if he does, they will almost certainly be very inaccurate and he may well lose the rhythm and timing of his action. Some great bowlers have been able to move the ball from leg by finger 'cut', but this is an advanced and most difficult technique. On the other hand, if his action is really good, it should help him to spin the ball from the off.

The ability to deceive a batsman by change of pace is particularly valuable because it is independent of the state of the pitch. The object of change of pace is to make the batsman play the wrong stroke to the ball or mistime the right stroke. For instance, he may have met three good length balls securely enough by a correctly played forward stroke, but if a fourth ball of the same length is bowled a little slower, the same forward stroke may lead to a catch in front of the wicket. Similarly, he may have played back comfortably to three balls of uniform length, but to a fourth, bowled a little faster, he may well be just too late and be bowled or l.b.w. If they are to deceive, such changes of pace must not be so pronounced as to 'signal themselves' to the batsman by alteration of run-up or delivery. The bowler must also learn how to alter the angle of his delivery to the batsman by making full use of the crease, i.e. how to bowl one ball from close to the wicket and another from just inside the return crease with accurate control of direction in each case: unless the batsman is alert enough to mark this and is really watching the ball, there is a chance that he may not play his stroke truly down the line of it.

If these are the resources which a medium-paced bowler must try to command, we may now consider the use he may make of them. Unless the scoreboard and the clock, or perhaps his captain, definitely dictate defensive strategy, he, like every other type of bowler, must set out to attack the batsmen. He must say to himself, 'I must get on top of this man by making him do what I want and must not allow him to do what he wants'. The first thing that a batsman wants in starting his innings or in facing a new bowler is 'to get a sight of the ball'. If a bowler bowls off the wicket, he is giving him a chance to do this without risk: so the first rule for the bowler is to bowl straight or at least straight enough to make him play at every ball.

But from the very start he must study the batsman's methods; he may even get some clue from his grip, his stance or his build. A tall man with a grip high up on the handle may well be looking for the chance to drive and be less at ease if forced to play off the back foot; a short, heavily built man with the right hand low on the handle is likely to favour back play, the hook and the cut, and may not like being made to play forward; a batsman with a very 'open' stance will invite the out-swinger directed at the off stump: a 'closed' stance might suggest the off-spinner or the in-swerve. In any case, an over or two should generally give the bowler some

Richie Benaud. Leg-spin: body sideways, wrist fully cocked and head looking down the wicket over the shoulder

48a

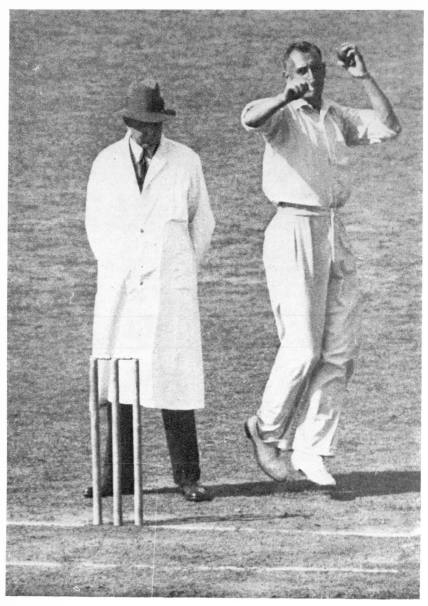

Hedley Verity. The cross-over stride; a study in balance and concentration

Hedley Verity. A perfect example of the follow-through against a braced front leg, with marked drag across the body.

Pat Pocock. A fine example of Position 2 in the basic action

idea of the type of batsman with whom he has to deal and he can regulate his attack and set his field accordingly.

The state of the pitch will, of course, also influence him. He may have to face the fact that it is giving him no help at all, that his off-break will not turn and that he must therefore rely mainly on swerve or on change of pace and tactical cunning: or he may find that it is slower than he would like and he may, therefore, have to push the ball through a little faster or a little farther up than usual in order that the batsman may be forced to play forward or at least prevented from playing back in comfort. Or again, he may find with delight that the pitch is really biting and that it asks for his off-break, supported by a reinforced leg-side field.

He must always be prepared to make such adjustments in his field according to the nature of the pitch and the type of batsman to whom he is bowling: but until absolutely forced to do so, they must be made on the basis of attack and not defence. At times he will find himself up against one batsman who is well set and attacking and another who is struggling. Remembering that as long as a batsman can be kept away from the bowling he is helpless, he must do all in his power to pin the latter down and not allow him by getting a single to give his partner the chance to assert himself. Here again the intelligent adjustment and co-operation of his field may be decisive.

When a good batsman on a good wicket has defied his opening attack long enough to look like really taking root, the bowler, provided that the scoreboard and clock justify it, is entitled to – indeed he must – take some chances. An off-driver may be presented with one or two perfect half-volleys on the off side as ground bait before being given another, a shade slower and rather wide, in the hope that he may sky it to cover or extra-cover. The cross-batted dispatch to the boundary of a half-volley on the middle and leg stumps may suggest another bowled a little faster and a little farther up. A natural cutter may be tempted with a ball short of a length just outside the off stump but appreciably faster in the hope that it may rise a little higher than usual. Only experience will teach a bowler how soon and how much he is entitled to experiment to get a wicket: how long will no doubt be decided by his captain. **But he must always remember that, the more difficult the wicket, the less justification there is for any experiment, and that the fewer runs there are to play with, the more he must rely on length, life and spin.**

Sometimes, of course, he will be forced by the state of the game, or ordered by his captain, to bowl defensively. It is then that control of direction, as well as of length, is so essential. In first-class cricket today many bowlers tend to direct their defensive bowling on or near the leg stump. But this demands a very high degree of accuracy and young bowlers will be far better advised to concentrate on the off side, for very few of the batsmen opposed to them will have an effective answer; their mishits will be more likely to go to hand and less likely to 'carry' for fours than if made on the on. Such defensive bowling should be supported by an inner and an outer ring of fieldsmen, the outer to stop the fours, the inner to save the singles; for it must always be remembered that four singles an over represent just over eighty runs an hour.

A final word may perhaps be said on the bowler's mental attitude. **His job demands just as much determination, just as much sustained concentration as the batsman's, and often a stouter heart.** A flying start must not betray him into over-confidence and any relaxation: still less must he allow punishment to 'rattle' or depress him. There will be days when he simply cannot bowl as well as he knows he should be able to: others when, though bowling better than he could hope, nothing will yet go right for him. In either case he must just go on trying, remembering always the bowler's ultimate consolation that, whereas for the batsman one ball can mean final eclipse, for him one ball can mean triumph.

SPIN BOWLING

This section is entitled 'Spin Bowling' rather than 'Slow Bowling' on the principle that most slow bowlers regard, and must regard, spin as the primary weapon of their attack. They must, of course, also hope to deceive the batsman in the air: to do so they must bowl slow enough to set him something of a problem in gauging the 'arc' of their flight, but not so slow that he can readily move out to the pitch of the ball and kill the break, or play it comfortably off the back foot if he stays at home. If, on the other hand, they try to bowl too fast they will lose this asset and very likely their length as well. In time, experience will teach them what pace suits their particular type of bowling best, how to vary this normal pace and, better still, how to 'flight' the ball in the true sense of the word; they must also aim to develop tactical skill.

There have been a few great slow bowlers who did not spin the ball much; perhaps they did not need to, such was their mastery of length, flight and tactical cunning. But **for most slow bowlers real power of spin is essential to success, and once a boy has made up his mind to become a spin bowler, he must never rest until he has acquired it.**

Like all other bowlers he must be grounded in the principles of the Basic Action, for by these alone can he hope to command control and life, whilst the proper use of his body in the delivery is a powerful reinforcement to spin. But **if the ball is to be really spun, the fingers and the wrist must do it and a boy must start learning how to make them do it at a very early stage.**

The mechanics of off- and leg-spin are analysed in the sections below devoted to those types of bowling. As soon as a boy has been grounded in the Basic Action he should be encouraged to experiment with and practice spin. He should begin to do this at quite short range and perhaps under-hand, gradually raising the height of his arm in delivery and increasing the range up to the length at which, according to his age, he will have to bowl in a match. He may start this practice with any sort of ball, provided that it is not too big and he can grip it properly: so long as the surface is true, the more responsive it is to spin, the better, for this will encourage him.

Sooner or later the coach must help him to decide whether he has the strength of finger, the flexibility of wrist and, perhaps, the imagination to warrant committing himself to the role of the genuine spin bowler. If he so decides, he must intensify his practice of spin and do everything he can to strengthen his fingers: even by himself he can do much by the constant squeezing and 'flipping' of any rubber ball.

He must also decide whether he is going to be an off-spinner or a leg-spinner. He will be very unwise to try to combine the two, for, if he is really to spin the ball, it is extremely difficult to bowl both breaks and at the same time to maintain consistency of action and therefore of length: but an even stronger reason is that it is impossible to set a satisfactory attacking field for both.

In making his choice he should weigh the following: the off-break is more 'natural' than the leg-break, less effort to bowl, and easier to combine with control of length and direction; moreover the general technique of the off-spin bowler is so closely allied with that of the medium-pace and even of the fast bowler that a boy who begins as the former may at a later stage switch over to one of the latter methods without any great readjust-ment; this is much less true for the leg-break bowler for whom a consider-able readjustment is necessary before he can bowl in any other style.

But if off-spin may seem to be the safer bet, leg-spin may well offer the greater prize. Though it is harder to bowl accurately, it operates more viciously and most batsmen are more fallible to it. This is particularly true of school cricket where a leg-spin bowler of any merit is worth his weight in gold; few school batsmen play leg-breaks convincingly, many commit early suicide to them, some are out to them almost before they go in. Nor is success in school cricket the highest prize to be won: records show con-clusively the decisive part often played by leg-spin bowlers in international cricket for fifty years and more.

It has nearly always been laid down as a cardinal rule that a bowler must first concentrate on learning to bowl a length before he starts practising spin or swerve. This is certainly true for bowling as a whole, but, as applied to leg-break bowling, it has recently been directly challenged by two of the foremost exponents of the art. They maintain that a boy who means to bowl leg-breaks must first concentrate on really spinning the ball and then learn to control his length. To support this view they argue, first: that to bowl a real leg-spinner demands a certain adjustment in the Basic Bowling

Action which cannot readily be made once that action has become automatic; and second: that to add length to leg-spin is in fact far easier than to add leg-spin to length. Probably one method will pay with one boy who is content to wait and work for his result, whilst the other is best for the boy who wants to be able to bowl leg-breaks reasonably well and as soon as possible. It is perhaps significant that some of the greatest spin-bowlers admit to having practised their spin long and intensively before attempting to bowl it in a match.

LEG-SPIN: TOP-SPIN: GOOGLY

The top-spinner and the googly are really developments of the leg-break and complementary to it. Both are very difficult balls to control, especially the googly which involves considerable strain on the arm and shoulder muscles.

Young boys should be strongly discouraged from over-bowling it: certainly they should practise it and the top-spinner, but even then they should stick mainly to the leg-break, remembering always that the value of the other two is mainly as surprise varieties to the latter. There is a real danger that if a boy gets 'bitten' with the googly and bowls it too much, the adjustment of action involved will become a habit and he will eventually find himself unable to spin his leg-break: he will then have exchanged his most dangerous ball for another which, except for the element of surprise, is easier to play: a very bad bargain.

The action

For the leg-break, as for all other types of bowler, a regular and rhythmic run-up which will bring him well-balanced to the crease is essential. **He should always bowl over the wicket,** for if he bowls 'round', the leg-break that pitches straight is more likely to miss the stumps and he cannot get an l.b.w. decision from any ball that pitches wide of the leg stumps: he is also more likely to bowl to leg from round than from over the wicket.

A proper pivot of the body in the delivery is of the first importance, for it will reinforce the flip of the wrist and the action of the fingers (see below) and will add to the ball's spin and pace off the ground.

The higher the action, the better the control of direction and the steeper the possible lift of the ball off the wicket.

The grip and the wrist

THE LEG-BREAK. The ball is 'bedded down' in the first three fingers spaced comfortably apart: the first two lie across the seam, their top joints taking

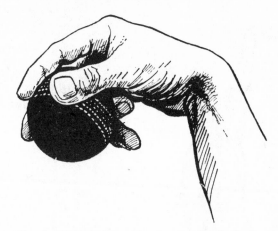

Fig. 4a. Grip for leg-spin: as seen by the batsman

Fig. 4b. Grip for leg-spin: as seen from behind the bowler

most of the pressure: the third and little fingers are curled below them so that
the top joint of the third finger, lying along the seam, presses hard upwards
against it: this third finger is the main lever for the spin: the thumb rests
naturally on the seam (Figs. 4a and 4b).

The wrist will be bent forward until the moment of release (Fig. 5a), **and,**
as the arm swings over, the palm of the hand will be facing the batsman or
perhaps fine-leg. As the ball is released, the third finger flicks outward towards
the batsman and the thumb downwards and away from him; at the same time
the wrist flips forward and the thumb and hand finish well across the body,
with the fingers stretched and pointing down the wicket (Fig. 5b).

THE TOP-SPINNER. The grip is the same as for the leg-break, but the
forward flip of the wrist begins just a little earlier so that the spin imparted to

Fig. 5a.
The leg-break:
the moment of delivery

Fig. 5b.
The leg-break:
follow-through

Fig. 6a.
The googly:
just after release

Fig. 6b. The googly:
follow-through

the ball by the flick of the third finger is directly down the line of the flight and
not towards the slips: at the moment of release the palm of the hand will be
facing mid-on: at the finish the arm and hand will be straight down the wicket.

THE GOOGLY. The grip is still the same, but the wrist turns over earlier
still and is bent back so that at the moment of release the back of the hand is
facing the batsman and the ball comes out over the top of the third and little
fingers (Fig. 6a). In order to do this, the left foot will land with the toe nearly
straight towards the batsman and parallel with the right foot: this will help
the essential dipping of the left shoulder. The follow-through of the bowling
arm is not across the body but straight down the wicket, and at the finish the
palm of the hand is often towards square-leg (Fig. 6b). By far the easiest way
to acquire the 'feel' of the goggly is to bowl it under-hand: it is as easy to
bowl under-hand as the leg-break.

TACTICS FOR THE LEG-SPIN BOWLER

Very few leg-spin bowlers have sufficient command of length and direction to justify their captain ever using them defensively: for such defensive bowling the medium-pace and the slow off-spin bowler is the natural choice. **The role of the leg-spinner is essentially to attack.**

He must bowl straight, preferably at the leg stump or just inside the pad – for most school batsmen are vulnerable there – and **he must keep the ball up,** for the ball that can be comfortably watched off the pitch and played off the back leg is no use, however much it turns.

His field must be stationed accordingly: this means that his infielders must be close enough to prevent singles, for otherwise he cannot hope to attack any batsman with a planned sequence of balls. On the other hand he must be prepared to invite the batsman to hit him, indeed he should want him to do so, and to do this with confidence he must have men out to save the fours. One of these deep-fields should be more or less straight behind him, and another may be deep, but not too deep, extra-cover for the catch from the ball which he will pitch well up to spin away from the off stump: but he should try to dispense with a wide long-on and by that inviting gap tempt the batsman to hit against the break. He would not be human if he did not sometimes bowl a long-hop and sometimes drop the ball on or outside the batsman's pads: he must, therefore, also have a deep-square-leg.

The faster and truer the pitch, the more he must try to 'give the ball room in the air', and to deceive the batsman by slight changes of pace and flight or by enticing him to chase the ball wide on the off. He must be prepared to experiment even at the cost of runs.

The deader the pitch, the more he must 'push the ball through' at the batsman, i.e. bowl a little faster, and not allow him to play it off the back foot.

On a really difficult pitch accuracy is everything: he must concentrate on length and direction, and his normal spin and the wicket should do the rest.

If he can bowl a googly, he should bowl it early on at each new batsman, for, if it does not dismiss him, it will start him looking for another which in fact may be a leg-break; but he should use it sparingly, for to bowl it too often may defeat its object and in doing so he may well lose his length for the leg-break: moreover his field cannot be set for both. The most promising target for the googly is the batsman who likes to push forward defensively and tends to 'leave the gate open' when he does so, or the back player who looks as if he does not know which way the ball is turning.

The top-spinner should be similarly used – for occasional surprise. It is particularly valuable on wickets off which the ball is turning sharply and against a batsman who is concentrating on back play or who is looking for the hook or playing across the ball on the leg stump: the more spin the wicket is taking, the greater the contrast and the threat of the top-spinner which slips through straight.

Of all the bowlers the leg-breaker has most need of an alert mind and an equable temperament. He is for ever pitting his wits against the batsman and must be always trying to detect his weaknesses and at the same time be prepared to play upon his strength, whether it be driving or hooking. He must realize that because he is a leg-spinner he is liable at times to be inaccurate and expensive. He must take the rough with the smooth, he must never mind being hit, he must never get rattled or give up trying, reminding himself that, if his is the most difficult of all bowling crafts, it is also perhaps the most intriguing, the most exciting and the most rewarding.

OFF-SPIN

Though most 'stock' bowlers normally command some degree of off-spin, cricket since the war has seen the emergence in increasing numbers of bowlers who are known specifically as 'off-spinners'. These men are stock bowlers, in the sense that they can be used on all types of wicket, and can bowl defensively as well as aggressively: but they get their name from the fact that they use off-spin more consistently and more effectively as their main weapon of attack. They vary, of course, in pace, but most of them find that to make their spin really bite on good wickets they must bowl on the slow side of medium. It is with this type of bowling that the present section is concerned.

The grip

Many of the illustrations of the grip for the off-break which appear in coaching manuals may well be misleading for boys, for they represent a grip, generally that of the bowling author, only possible for a full-grown hand and often only for a hand with exceptionally long fingers. Length and strength of finger are great assets for spinning the ball, for spin depends on leverage; but even if a boy's hand is slightly smaller than normal, he should not feel that he cannot spin the ball, and what is here written of the grip should not be impracticable for him.

Whereas for the leg-spin and the googly the third finger is the most important, for off-spin it is the first two fingers and, with most bowlers, especially the first. The first finger will lie along the seam with the top joint slightly bent and biting into the near edge of it: the second finger will be spaced well, but not uncomfortably, away from the first, with the two other fingers curled below in natural support and the thumb in a corresponding position on the other side of the ball.

Many off-spin bowlers prefer to place their first two fingers across the seam with the top joints gripping it (Fig. 7). In either grip the farther the two

M.C.C.—5

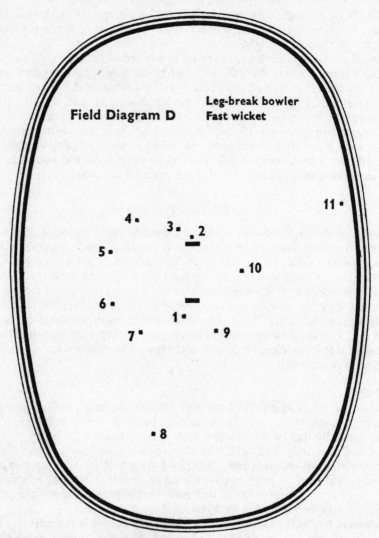

Field Diagram D

Leg-break bowler
Fast wicket

1. Bowler   4. Third-man   7. Mid-off   10. Mid-wicket
2. Wicket-keeper   5. Cover-point   8. Long-off   11. Deep-square-leg
3. Slip   6. Extra-cover   9. Mid-on

Slip will be rather wider than normal and well up. The deep-leg fieldsman will be behind rather than in front of the wicket, as on a fast pitch the ball is more likely to be swept than hooked.

If the bowler is sure of his length and feels that he is 'on top' he may bring third-man up to second-slip, and mid-off close in to the batsman: long-off will then take mid-off's place but should be as deep as possible provided always that he can save the single.

A bowler who can bowl a googly and finds it really turning may prefer to have another short-leg rather than a second-slip or short-mid-off.

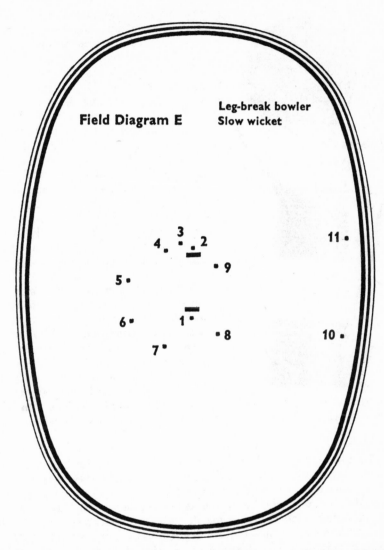

Field Diagram E **Leg-break bowler**
Slow wicket

1. Bowler	4. Second-slip	7. Mid-off	10. Deep-mid-wicket
2. Wicket-keeper	5. Cover-point	8. Mid-on	11. Deep-backward-
3. Slip	6. Extra-cover	9. Short-leg	square-leg

Short-leg and slip must be closer than on a hard wicket.
If the ball is turning and lifting and the bowler's length is accurate, he may bring up cover to rather wide and short-mid-off.

first fingers can with comfort be spaced apart, the greater the leverage they can apply: the degree of spin can in fact be varied by altering the spacing of them. The thumb will rest lightly against the side of the ball: some bowlers with large hands, long fingers and wide spread between the index and second fingers detach it altogether.

Boys with small hands may find it easier to bed the ball more into the base of the fingers and to make the second finger the main spinning lever. Some bowlers have found that with this grip the ball will occasionally swing away and this, especially to the good batsman, is perhaps the most dangerous ball that an off-spinner can deliver.

For an off-break the ball must be spun clockwise, i.e. from left to right, and the action of the hand is much the same as in turning the knob to open a door: the wrist will turn outwards and,

Fig. 7. Grip for off-spin

as it does so, the two first fingers and especially the first, will drag the seam outwards and downwards: as the wrist turns, the hand flips forwards and downwards, finishing with palm upwards and the thumb pointing more or less straight down the pitch.

The action

The adjustments which may be made in the Basic Bowling Action to increase off-spin are slight but definite. The right arm may be taken back rather more behind the right thigh before it starts its upward swing. **The wrist should at this point be fully cocked and opened as much as possible so that the thumb points slightly to the off side of the bowler's umpire: the palm will thus face directly upwards. The left foot in the delivery stride should be taken slightly across the line of delivery. The initial sideways turn of the body should be somewhat accentuated and its unwinding should be delayed so that the ball is delivered with the maximum 'drag' across the body (Fig. 8). A high action is desirable for off-spinners,** for the lower the arm, the more must the natural line of the ball's flight counteract the spin.

The initial sideways turn of the body should be somewhat accentuated and its unwinding should be delayed as long as possible. To help spin and

flight, the ball should be bowled with
the maximum drag across the pitch
and should be delivered just as the arm
is passing the head.

TACTICS FOR THE OFF-SPINNER

On a true, fast wicket very few young
bowlers can hope to turn the ball
enough from off or to be accurate
enough in length to justify their bowling
round the wicket to a leg-side field.

Unless the ball is really turning it
is not likely to be edged much to his
close in leg-traps and, unless he is
really accurate, the latter, if they are
close enough to warrant their name,
are exposed to real risk of injury.
Moreover the less skilful the batsman,
the better chance he has of getting
runs from the ball on or outside the
leg stump, even if a good length, as
opposed to the ball on or outside the
off stump.

The bowler should, therefore, under
these conditions, direct his line of
attack just outside the off stump and
set his field accordingly, thus forcing
the batsman to take risks if he tries to
avoid the arc covered by the fielders.

*Fig. 8. The off-break:
just after release*

He will hope to wear the batsman down by accuracy or deceive him by
some device, for instance by the ball which he does not try to spin at all
and which goes straight on, by a change of pace, or by 'flight'.

The object of change of pace, of which something has been said in the
section on Medium-pace Bowling, is to deceive the batsman as to when the
ball will reach him; by what is called 'flighting' the ball the bowler is out to
delude him as to where it will pitch, in other words to make the ball look
as if it will drop farther up than in fact it will. The simplest method of doing
this is for him to deliver the ball, at his normal pace but with a slightly
higher trajectory, from two feet, or even a yard, behind the bowling crease.
Another method is by letting go of the ball rather earlier than usual in his
normal delivery, i.e. just before his hand reaches the vertical, or by slightly
dropping the level of his bowling arm: in each case the ball will have just

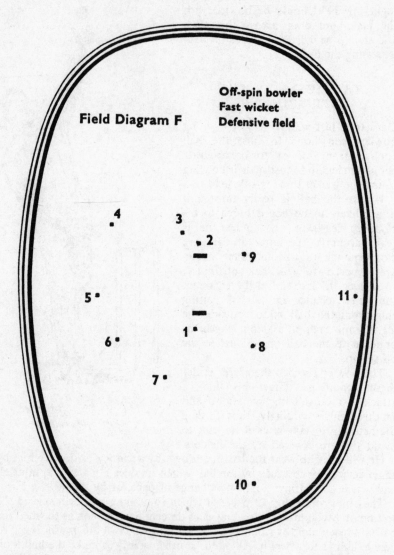

Field Diagram F

**Off-spin bowler
Fast wicket
Defensive field**

1. Bowler	4. Short-third-man	7. Mid-off	10. Long-on
2. Wicket-keeper	5. Cover-point	8. Mid-on	11. Deep-mid-wicket
3. Slip	6. Extra-cover	9. Square-leg	

If opposed to a strong driver the bowler may have to drop mid-off back to save four; long-on can then be stationed rather wider.

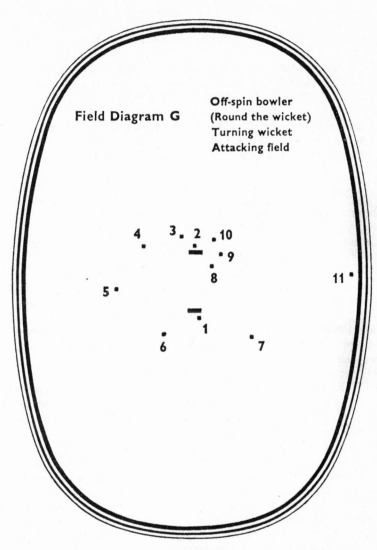

Field Diagram **G**

Off-spin bowler
(Round the wicket)
Turning wicket
Attacking field

1. Bowler	5. Cover-point	9. Short-leg
2. Wicket-keeper	6. Mid-off	10. Leg-slip
3. Slip	7. Deep-wide-mid-on	11. Deep-square-leg
4. Short-square-third-man	8. Forward-short-leg	

As the bowler is bowling round the wicket, mid-off will be rather straighter and mid-on rather wider.

that extra distance to travel in the air. One of the greatest of all slow bowlers used to say that when he flighted the ball, he had the feeling of his first finger sliding through underneath the ball and 'leaving it behind'.

The young bowler must experiment for himself to find out which of these various suggestions are effective for him, but he must realize that all of them, even the first, need hard work and constant practice and that 'flight' must never be pursued at the expense of length.

In general it may be said that the better the pitch the more he must rely on beating the batsman in the air rather than off the ground, and that to do this he will tend to bowl a little slower than what he feels to be his normal pace.

Should he find himself forced to bowl defensively, he will bowl wider with corresponding adjustment of his field. In fact his tactics, whether in attack or defence, will largely conform with those already outlined for the medium-paced bowler.

On a true pitch it will be only to left-handed batsmen that he should bowl from round the wicket.

It is when the pitch is crumbling or sticky that the off-spinner comes into his own and may hope to play a decisive part in the match. His spin should now really bite, and the ball turn sharply and at times 'check' and get up. **Under these conditions he will bowl round the wicket. By doing so he will greatly increase his chance of getting batsmen l.b.w., for an off-break which, if bowled over the wicket, would miss the stumps, can, if bowled round the wicket, hit them (Fig. 9).**

The arc of his field will now be different and concentrated more on the leg side: but he must not allow this to make him feel that his line of attack should be directed at the middle and leg stumps; he should bowl at, or slightly outside the off stump, remembering that the more the pitch is taking spin, the more will any ball that pitches straight tend to miss the wicket.

He should bowl slightly faster than he would on a true pitch and his aim will be to bring the batsman pushing forward on his front leg. Accuracy of length is all important, for he cannot afford to intersperse his length balls with long-hops and full-pitches, if he is to expect his leg-traps to field close enough to make catches from defensive strokes or to have the confidence so necessary for them in their 'front line' role.

To sustain this accuracy the less experienced bowler may well have to resist the temptation to bowl slightly faster or to put maximum spin on the ball, for an attempt to do so may lead to his bowling short, **and to bowl short is the worst of all sins on a sticky wicket.** In these conditions direction is almost as important as length: the bowler must make the batsman play: balls on or outside his legs can be ignored if he is defending, whilst if he is attacking they invite the cross-bat hit off which about the only chance for a wicket lies in a probably difficult catch to deep-square or deep-long leg.

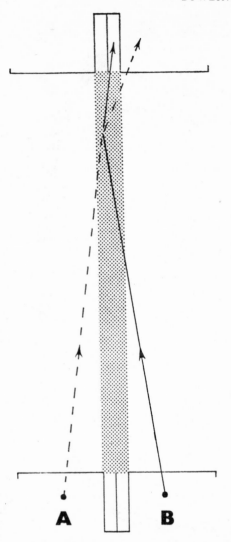

Fig. 9.
An off-break bowled (a) over
and (b) round the wicket.
The point of pitch and degree
of turn are identical

A   **B**

The slower the wicket, the farther up must the bowler pitch the ball: the
muddier it is, the more pains he must take to keep the ball, and especially
its seam, clean.

LEFT-HAND BOWLING

The principles of the Basic Action are, *mutatis mutandis,* exactly the same
for left-hand bowlers as for right-hand, but the former differ from the

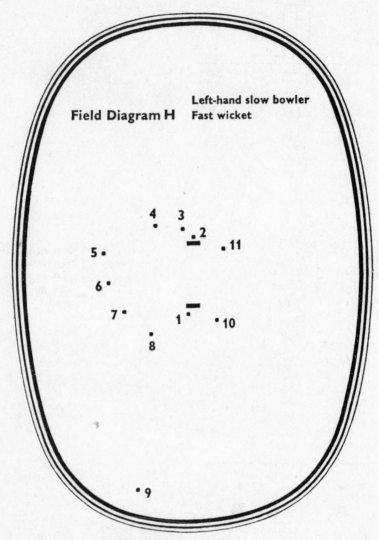

Field Diagram H   Left-hand slow bowler
                        Fast wicket

1. Bowler	4. Third-man	7. Second-extra-cover	10. Mid-on
2. Wicket-keeper	5. Cover	8. Mid-off	11. Short-leg
3. Slip	6. Extra-cover	9. Long-off	

If the batsman is being kept on the defensive, long-off may be brought in to short mid-off (in which case mid-off can be stationed rather deeper and straighter), or alternatively to short-leg behind the wicket.

If the batsman is driving strongly on the off side, one of the off-side fielders will be dropped back to save four and the others adjusted accordingly.

latter in two fundamentals, their 'natural' swing is into the right-hand batsman, their 'natural' break is away from him. Until a comparatively recent date in cricket history, all left-hand bowlers, bowling to right-hand batsmen, have bowled round the wicket: this, of course, still holds good for the slow or slow-medium bowler on wickets that will take spin: a possible exception will be when there is 'rough' close to the line of the leg stump or when he is bowling to left-handers, or when there is a wind from the direction of fine leg which may help him to drift an occasional ball away. But today the medium or faster left-hand bowler more often than not bowls over the wicket. From this angle, and directing his line of attack at the middle and off stumps, he is making the best of both worlds, and presenting the batsman with a double problem: for though his natural tendency will be to swing the ball in, the basic line of his trajectory will be from leg to off, and his swinging ball is less likely to finish wide of the leg stump, whilst the one that does not swing will be 'leaving the batsman' who may well play inside it.

The setting of the field for such a bowler must inevitably present a problem. As long as the ball is really moving in the air, he will have an attacking field, inevitably to some extent split between the off and on sides. But if the ball is not moving much, or if the batsman seems to be getting on top and finding the gaps in the field, he must make up his mind how he means to bowl, i.e. primarily 'inwards' at the wicket, or 'outwards' at and outside the off stump, and then must set his field accordingly.

The most common, and indeed by tradition (especially in Yorkshire!) the classical type of left-hand bowler is the orthodox slow or slow-medium who relies on spin and flight or change of pace. On good true wickets he cannot hope to turn the ball as much as the 'wrist-spinner', but should certainly be far more accurate: his line of attack will be at and outside the off stump, with a predominantly off-side field: though, like every other bowler, he will hope to attack, he may well find himself at times forced to bowl defensively with an inner and outer ring of fielders, the former to stop, as far as possible, the short single, the latter to cut off the fours. Length and varying arc of flight will be his armour, and he must be prepared on occasions to 'buy' his wickets by tempting the batsman to drive the slower and wider short half-volley. It is probably true that the less help he is getting from the wicket, the more desirable it is for him to deliver the ball from as near the stumps as possible rather than from wide on the crease.

But it is when the ball is really turning that such a bowler should hope to prove a match winner. He will now bowl at the middle stump, more or less abandon experiment in flight, and concentrate on length and his natural spin: he must at all costs keep the ball up, and regard any delivery which the batsman can play comfortably off the back foot as a crime. Ideally he should be able to bowl to a silly-mid-off, a gully, one or even

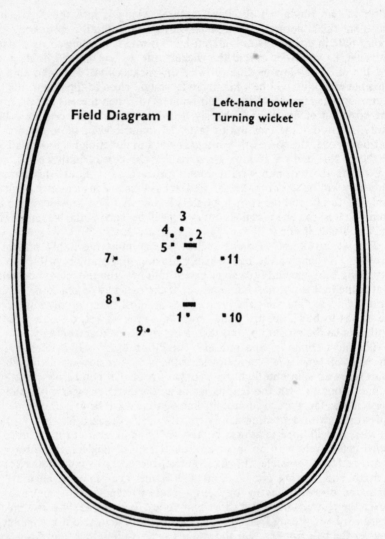

Field Diagram I   Left-hand bowler
Turning wicket

1. Bowler	4. Gully	7. Cover-point	10. Mid-on
2. Wicket-keeper	5. Point	8. Extra-cover	11. Forward-short-**leg**
3. Slip	6. Short-mid-off	9. Mid-off	

*This field assumes that the ball is turning sharply and that the bowler is really accurate
and is pinning the batsman down.*

*If the batsman counter-attacks, the bowler may be forced to drop his extra-cover to
rather wide long-off, replacing him by short mid-off: he may also prefer to drop gully or
point back to rather short third-man for the catch or the mis-hit from the breaking ball.*

two slips, and a close in short-leg for the occasional ball that may go on in with his arm. As always he must regard this field as elastic, and be prepared, but only if so forced by the batsman, to dispense with his short mid-off, or one of his slips. He should never need a deep-square-leg: the more sharply he can turn the ball, the wider will his slips and gully be stationed.

The tactics of the abnormal left-hander, who bowls the wrist-spun 'Chinaman' turning in to the batsman, will correspond with those of the right-hand off-spinner: he will bowl at or just outside the off stump to a reinforced on-side field, but a slip is essential for the ball which he must hope the batsman will edge off his googly or from the one that goes straight on: to a left-hand batsman he will aim at the middle and leg stump, with one or two slips according to how much he is turning the ball and a gully: he will also need a close in short-leg for his googly.

4

Batting

The main object of this section of the book is to analyse the principles of technique which must always be the basis of good batsmanship: but the successful operation of that technique will hinge on other factors.

Of these the most important is that which is commonly termed 'ball sense', the ability to sight the ball and judge its length quickly and then deal with it effectively: closely allied to this is that indefinable something called 'timing' and the ease of physical co-ordination which makes it possible. This 'ball sense', though it can to some extent be developed, is in the main a natural gift: an experienced coach may sense it, or the lack of it, almost at his first sight of a boy with a bat in his hands. Some boys have not got it at all: most of these will probably not want to play cricket and it is very doubtful whether they should be made to do so, for to them cricket may well be a waste of time and a vexation of spirit: **but there are others of them who, though with no natural gift, long to be cricketers; for these no coaching effort is too great or more repaying, for the spirit that is in them deserves the reward of whatever success they may be helped to attain.**

Of those really gifted with this 'ball sense' no more need be said than that they owe it to themselves and their coach to make the most of it.

But by far the majority are those who have some ability to deal with the ball but need all the help that can be given them to make the best of it: given that help and the willingness to avail themselves of it, most of them can become at least competent batsmen: it is with these that the coach's main work lies.

The next factor to be considered is not physical at all: it may be bluntly defined as character: it plays a large part in batting and the coach must try to instil and develop it.

No doubt, what is commonly known as 'match temperament', the instinct to welcome and rise to a big occasion, is in the main a natural gift: but a great deal can be done to build up the right attitude of mind and will in the batsman and to make him realize that it is an essential reinforcement to technique.

Too much stress cannot be laid on the importance of concentration at the

wicket and the hard work necessary to build up that habit of mind. Batting really consists of playing one ball at a time, and the batsman has to learn to key himself up before each ball is bowled to the maximum of vigilance and determination. A very great batsman used to say that he reckoned it took him at least a fortnight's regular net practice at the start of the season before he felt that he was really looking at the ball! The coach must rub into his boys how important it is to work at this habit of concentration by a sustained effort of will in every innings which they play, whether at the nets or in the middle: he will remind them how one lapse in vigilance, one stupid or careless stroke, may cost them their wicket and even their side a victory. Most young cricketers who mean business will at least start their innings with some concentration, but it tends to evaporate as the runs come and as they feel that they have to some extent justified themselves. The coach must persuade them that the more they feel themselves well set, the more criminal it is to get out through carelessness or over-confidence, and that even if they reach 50, the applause that greets it should be a signal to them to metaphorically 'take guard' again and, of course, always with an eye on the clock and the score, to start in to get 50 more.

The more they realize that their duty, first, last and all the time, is to their side and not to themselves, the more will this resolution both at the start and throughout their innings be reinforced.

Confidence is a great factor in batting temperament, and to some extent this too is, or is not, part of a boy's natural make-up. In a few, especially after a run of success, it may need tempering, though in the long run the game itself will look after that, but with the majority it needs constant building up.

However critical a coach may feel it necessary to be at practice or in a talk after a match, the overall note of his coaching must be encouragement. Especially is this necessary before an important match: at the last practice for it, he will be wise to avoid much technical criticism and concentrate on reinforcing each batsman's belief in himself. He must, like Caesar of old, encourage his men to 'remember their former prowess' and to believe that they can win.

If on the eve of it his best batsman is conscious of a recent run of failures and an unnerving lack of form at his last net, the coach must remind him that even the greatest players have often felt the same and have suddenly broken through to play a match-winning innings.

No daunting reputation of the opposition's bowlers must be allowed to make a boy forget that, as has been said, batting consists of playing one ball at a time, no matter by whom it is bowled, and that a stout heart, concentration and a sound batting method must sooner or later bring their reward in runs.

A good coach will somehow manage to make his batsmen feel that the more formidable the enemy, the more inspiring is the challenge, calling for just that extra bit of determination from every man in the team which may make the difference between victory and defeat.

Then there is the factor which may be called 'cricket sense', the faculty of deciding rightly what tactics to pursue in any given situation and against any given bowler, when to take some risk and when to concentrate on defence, of judging how best to counter some particular setting of the field or some special difficulty of the wicket. This must, of course, come mainly by experience but the good coach can help his boys to acquire it by explaining to them the lessons to be learnt from each day's play and the importance to a batsman of really giving his mind to his batting. He must try to make them understand that **even the champions are always learning.**

The last reinforcement to be harnessed to a proper technique is the offensive spirit. To win matches a batsman must make runs: though a sound defence is necessary if he is to stay long at the crease, his purpose must be, wherever and as soon as possible, to wrest the initiative from the bowler and retain it.

Obviously some boys are, by temperament and natural gift, more disposed to attack than others; but the coach must aim at developing some attacking strokes in all his pupils and above all at instilling in them the will to attack.

The greatest problem in the teaching of batting is how to impart the inevitably artificial technique of straight-bat play and at the same time, so far from curbing, positively to foster a boy's natural instinct to hit the ball and enjoy hitting it.

To cramp boys with purely defensive technique, still more to curb their offensive spirit, is the worst of coaching sins.

In cricket, as in other games, genius may often seem to defy normally accepted rules: but in fact it succeeds in spite of, not because of, its unorthodoxy and conforms much more than may be apparent to the basic principles of style.

It is now getting on for 200 years since the bowler began to try to 'pitch a length' and the batsman discovered, and began to put into practice, the only logical answer to it and the first principle of his art, that **the longer the full face of the bat is on the line of the ball the better chance he has of meeting it.** No matter what changes in stroke play there have been since then and may be in the future, it has been, and must always be, true that the straight bat moving down the line of the ball is the basis of good batting.

By far the most important, and the most difficult, task of any coach in batting is to train the young batsman to play straight: to this end, he should encourage him to strengthen his left hand by every means in his power, for it is the left hand that must control every straight-bat stroke.

Unfortunately this is not the natural method of hitting a ball, for it demands that the left or top hand should control the bat, whereas in the 'natural man' the right or bottom hand always tends to dominate.

N.B. Everything that follows is written for a right-hand batsman: for a left-hander reverse 'left' and 'right'.

GRIP

A correct grip is of great importance if the hands are to work together and so ensure control and power in playing strokes on both sides of the wicket.

The following two methods are suggested as useful in securing a natural grip:

(*a*) The batsman should place the bat face downwards on the ground with the handle facing him and then stoop down and pick it up with both hands as if it was a club which he meant to put to immediate use.

(*b*) He should place the bat with the face towards him so that the top of the handle rests in the fork of his legs, and then take hold of it naturally with both hands.

In either case he should find that:

(i) **The hands are close together with the left hand near the top of the handle.**

(ii) **The back of the left hand, if the bat is held upright, faces somewhere between mid-off and extra cover.**

(iii) **The fingers and thumb of both hands are well round the handle.**

Fig. 1.
Grip:
hands close together:
Vs of the hands on same
line, half-way between
outside edge and splice

M.C.C.—6

Fig. 2.
Grip: as seen by the bowler: left hand is cushioned comfortably against inside of left thigh; back of hand, so positioned, faces bowler

(iv) **The V formed by the first finger and thumb of the left hand is directly over the corresponding V of the right, and the line of these V's is half-way between the outer edge of the bat and the splice (Figs. 1 and 2).**

TAKING GUARD

The object in taking guard is to enable the batsman to know exactly where he is in relation to the wicket, especially the leg stump. His guard should ensure that the toes of both feet are just outside the line of that stump and that his head is looking down a line straight between the wickets. A batsman with a naturally upright stance may prefer a 'two leg', i.e. middle and leg stumps guard. If he is inclined to stoop over in his stance he will certainly be safer with leg stump. In asking for a guard he should hold the bat upright with its face to the umpire who can then see clearly which stump or stumps it will be covering. It is quite unnecessary to dig a pit with the bat after taking guard. All the batsman needs is to make a mark to show him where he stands relative to the leg stump. He will expect, and if necessary ask, the umpire to give him guard from a point directly behind and over the bowler's wicket: that is the line by which the umpire will adjudge him out or not out l.b.w. To ask him for guard 'from where the bowler bowls' makes no sense at all.

STANCE

An easy, relaxed and balanced stance is important, for the back-lift and all strokes spring from it. It conditions the proper watching of the ball and the proper movement of the feet.

The stances of batsmen in fact vary widely in detail, and no boy should be forced to stand in a way which he finds at all unnatural or uncomfortable. But most first-class batsmen conform in general to the following principles:

The feet

(i) The heels should be some three to six inches apart, with the popping crease between them. The right foot should be parallel with, or pointing just behind, the crease and the left foot roughly parallel with it, though many batsmen find it more natural to point it more towards cover and indeed deliberately open their 'stance' when facing in-swing or off-spin bowling. The toes of both feet should be just clear of the line of the leg stump.

(ii) **The weight should be equally balanced between, and very slightly on the front part of, the feet.**

(iii) The knees should be very slightly relaxed, making for easy and quick movement.

(iv) There should be no movement of the feet until the length of the ball is judged and the actual stroke begins.

The body

The body should face as squarely to point as is consistent with comfort: the more directly the left shoulder can point at the opposite wicket, the easier will be the correct and straight back-lift, but this must on no account be exaggerated or the stance will become artificial and strained.

The head

The head must be kept upright and turned towards the bowler with the eyes as level as possible; only so can the batsman focus both eyes together and command a proper sight and judgment of the ball; it must be kept as still as possible.

The expression 'two-eyed stance' is nonsense: every good batsman has both his eyes full to the ball. It is the 'two-shoulder stance', where feet and

Fig. 3.
The stance:
as seen by the bowler

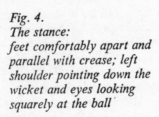

Fig. 4.
The stance:
feet comfortably apart and
parallel with crease; left
shoulder pointing down the
wicket and eyes looking
squarely at the ball

shoulders open up towards the bowler, that makes for a faulty back-lift and cross-bat play.

The bat

Most players find it natural and comfortable to ground the bat just behind the toes of the right foot but just to the off side of them, with the blade facing the left leg and the hands at ease just away from or even touching the left thigh. But here again the great thing is that the batsman should feel comfortable and 'at the ready' (Figs. 3 and 4).

THE BACK-LIFT

The back-lift must never be thought of as preliminary to and distinct from the stroke, but as an initial and vital part of it.

A correct back-lift is not 'natural' and too much attention cannot be paid to getting it right.

Though it is true that many gifted batsmen lift the bat back in something of a 'loop', they so adjust it that in all straight back strokes the bat starts its downward movement at the top of the line of the intended stroke. For straight balls that movement will begin from a point directly above the wicket; the wider the ball is to the off and the wider the stroke is aimed, the more must the initial turn of the left shoulder start the downward movement of the bat from the direction of fine leg; for balls on, or just outside the leg stump, the dipping and opening of the left shoulder will start the downward movement of the bat from the line of slip.

The principle must hold good that the straighter the back-lift is in relation to the line of the intended stroke, the better must be the prospect of the whole stroke being played straight. The bat should be taken back mainly by the left hand, the left elbow bending and the left arm being pushed back far enough to give a slight feeling of tension in the left shoulder, and the left wrist 'cocking' and thus naturally opening the face of the bat towards point. The control of the left hand and arm is essential. If the right hand takes charge it will tend to take the bat back towards third man and open the body towards the bowler; the grip of this hand should in fact be relaxed into a thumb and finger hold. If both hands are pushed slightly away from the body, it will help to ensure that the left shoulder is kept pointing down the pitch (Figs. 5 and 6).

Though at the start of a batsman's innings, especially against fast bowling on a fast wicket, some reduction of the normal back-lift may be advisable, coaches should be very chary of discouraging a naturally free back-lift. Nearly all the great batsmen pick the bat well up and, and though it is true that they commit themselves later to their stroke and yet have time in which to play it, the average player will find that the late back-lift will find that the late back-lift will almost certainly tend to produce a hurried and warped stroke.

Fig. 5.
The back-lift at the start of the
forward stroke:
the left shoulder and arm have
pushed the bat back over the top of
the stumps and the left wrist has
opened the face of the bat:
the head is poised looking full down
the wicket

Fig. 6.
The back-lift at the start of
a back stroke:
the poise of the body is still
forward

Common faults

Grip. (i) Having the hands too far apart, with right hand too low on the handle. This prevents the hands from working in unison as is necessary in all straight-bat strokes, and encourages the right hand to take charge and to warp the line of the stroke.

(ii) Having the back of the left hand behind the handle. This makes a full follow-through impossible.

Stance. (i) Feet too far apart: this prejudices initial movement.

(ii) Stance too 'open': this encourages a crooked back-lift and makes it more difficult to lead with the left shoulder on the off-side.

(iii) Head not sufficiently turned to face down the wicket, or taken too far over to the off-side, with the eyes consequently not focusing the ball together.

Back-lift. (i) Right hand too much in control.

(ii) Right elbow kept tucked into the side.

(iii) Picking the bat up late and thus hurrying and probably warping the stroke.

THE FORWARD AND BACK STROKES

These two strokes constitute the basis of all batting, whether in attack or defence; indeed all cricket strokes are really adaptations of one or the other.

The greatest change in batting technique that has taken place in the last sixty years is to be found in the development of back play. Whereas in the 'nineties, nine out of ten first-class batsmen would tend to push forward to meet the ball of awkward length, the majority today will play it off the back foot, thereby enabling themselves to watch it off the pitch; the more difficult the wicket and the more the ball is turning, the more do they rely on their back play, unless, of course, they are able to smother it by playing right forward with a dead bat.

This revolution – for it is nothing less – has certainly led to a great strengthening in defence, but only at a price. The modern predisposition to play back has inevitably operated against the playing of those attacking strokes off the front foot which constitute, whether for the player of the spectator, so much of the glory of the game, and the lack of which allows the bowler to wrest and maintain the initiative. Most great batsmen have been ready and able to play off the front and back foot with equal facility. The coach must never allow the importance of back play to dominate a boy's outlook on batting to the exclusion of forward play; nor must a boy be allowed to think of defence in terms of back play and of attack in terms of forward. Both strokes can be played either defensively or offensively, but the groove of the bat's movement, whether curtailed in defence or lengthened and accelerated in attack, is the same and the mastery of this technique is the essential foundation for batting.

These strokes will first be analysed as played defensively, because their basic mechanism can thus be more easily understood and practised. But in teaching the back and forward strokes the coach must drive it home that he is not only offering the means of defence without which no batsman can hope to be consistently successful, but also the mechanism for that attack into which every batsman must hope to pass as soon as and whenever he gets the chance.

THE FORWARD STROKE

The forward stroke is really one and the same whether played straight, to the off or to the on: the only difference is in the position of the left foot and the line upon which the head and left shoulder move out on to the ball.

The head

In all forward strokes the left shoulder with the left side of the head close to it, must lead out and on to the line of the ball. All the great batsmen 'lead with the shoulder and head'. If only boys can be taught to think of this, they will find that their left foot and the balance of their body weight must automatically follow.

The eyes must watch – really watch – the ball as nearly on to the bat as is possible: the head should be just in front of the left foot.

The left foot

The left foot will move out, to land heel first, as far as possible towards the pitch of the ball and as near as possible to its line. The nearer it can get to the pitch, the less room there is for the ball to alter direction after pitching: the nearer it can get to the line, the less gap will there be between bat and leg.

The left knee must bend slightly to allow the weight of the body to come through into the stroke and to 'shut the gate' between bat and leg. For straight balls the toe of the left foot will point approximately towards extra-cover. The wider the ball is to the off, the wider will the left toe point.

For balls on the leg stump or on the inside of the pads the left foot will open up to point more directly down the wicket. Boys will find this much the most difficult problem in the forward stroke but if they can master it they will find that it goes a long way to solving the problem of on-side play. Unless the left foot thus opens up, it is impossible for the weight of the body to move through on to the line of the stroke, i.e. in the general direction of mid-on.

Peter May. The stance: head fully turned down the wicket and eyes level

Colin Cowdrey. Feet parallel with the crease: left shoulder pointing down the wicket

80a

W. G. Grace. The back-lift: the face of the bat is fully open; the position of the head and shoulder is perfect; the right hand has slipped down the handle for a defensive back-stroke

80b

Colin Cowdrey. The back-lift before a drive: the left arm is clearly in control and the head and left shoulder are leading into the stroke.

Jack Hobbs. The start of a quick-footed off-drive: the left shoulder and hip are leading the attack

The right foot

The heel of the right foot will naturally ease to allow the weight of the body to come forward on to the left foot: at the end of the stroke only the toe of the right foot will be on the ground.

The left shoulder and left hip

The position of the left shoulder is fundamental to all correct forward strokes. It should point down the line of the intended stroke.

The wider the stroke is aimed to the off, the more should the back of the shoulder be turned on the bowler. This initial movement of 'turning the back' for the off-drive is noticeable in most of the greatest exponents of that stroke.

For strokes aimed at or wide of mid-on, the shoulder and hip should lead in that direction but must never be allowed to fall away from the stroke, for this will at once pull the bat across the line of the ball.

The hands

The left hand must grip the bat very firmly and control the whole shape of the stroke (Fig. 7).

At the moment of impact the back of the left hand will point towards extra-cover or mid-off: the left wrist will be bent and the top of the bat handle will be seen in the angle of the wrist. The left hand will be slightly in advance of the right: this ensures the ball being kept down.

The right hand will, as the bat comes forward, relax its grip into one between the thumb and the first two fingers. It is impossible to play any defensive forward stroke correctly if the bat continues to be gripped in the palm of the right hand.

The bat

The longer the full face of the bat is on the path of the ball, the more secure must be the stroke.

When the stroke is played defensively, i.e. to balls of a good length, the bat will meet the ball as near its pitch as the forward stride will allow and appreciably in front of the toe of the left foot. There will be no follow-through; the full face of the bat will remain held on the line of the ball. (Fig. 8).

The most common faults are:
(i) Not leading with the head and left shoulder out on to the line of the ball.
(ii) Not taking the left foot far enough forward, and not bending the left knee.
(iii) Not making the left hand and arm control the stroke.
(iv) Not moving the full face of the bat along the line of the ball.
(v) Not meeting the ball in front of the left foot.

Fig. 7.
The forward stroke:
head and eyes full on the line of the
ball, left shoulder, arm, and hand in
control, presenting full face of the bat:
left knee slightly bent to 'shut the
gate'

Fig. 8. The forward stroke: the batsman has made full use of his reach: bat meets ball just in front of the left foot and virtually below the eyes

THE DRIVES

The player who cannot drive is only half a batsman. Not only does he lack the most exhilirating and productive weapon of attack, but, as he lacks it, he greatly simplifies the bowler's task and enables him to win and hold the initiative by keeping the ball well up. Conversely, a batsman who can drive, especially if he can use his feet, can wrest that initiative from the bowler, and, by inducing him to bowl short, greatly simplify the problem of his own defence, especially on slow and turning wickets. This is also inevitably reflected in the placing of the field; if, by his ability and readiness to drive, the batsman can force the bowler to place one or more men in the deep field he makes it impossible for him to maintain a network of close-set attacking fielders.

The general mechanism of the drive is really the same as that of the forward stroke, but operating on an extended and accelerated arc. As in the forward stroke, the head and left shoulder will lead, the left hip will be kept up to the intended line of the stroke, and the left arm will control the arc. But the arc of the drive will begin with a freer and higher back-lift, will be kept as long and flat as possible with both arms following right through until, before the natural brake of the wrists, they and the bat are pointing after the ball in a straight line.

Power in driving comes from the continuation of this long arc and the acceleration of it by the forearms, wrists and hands just before impact.

The longer the blade of the bat is kept on the path of the ball the better, and this is facilitated if the left arm is kept as close to the body as possible in the back swing, and the right arm as close as possible as the bat comes through. In the timed acceleration of the arc the right arm powerfully reinforces the left, but on no account must the right shoulder be allowed to warp the line of the stroke, or the right hand to shut the face of the bat before impact.

For drives along the ground the ball will be met at a point just outside the left toe and more or less under the head, but all really good drivers have been able and ready to drive the ball in the air over the head of the bowler, mid-off or mid-on, and for this lofted drive the ball must be met earlier, i.e. at a point beyond the left foot.

Against bowling of quick or medium pace the drive will normally be played with one stride: but when the ball is slow and its trajectory high enough to give the batsman time, he can drive 'quick-footed', moving down the pitch in a smooth *chassé*: **in this the right foot will work up behind the left, thus keeping the left shoulder up to the ball and preventing the weight from falling away from the stroke; this movement must be kept as smooth as possible in order that the head may remain level and so continue to focus the ball accurately (Figs. 9a and 9b).**

Fig. 9a.
Moving out to drive:
following the first stride, the
right foot has moved up just
behind the left foot, thus enabling
the left shoulder to keep leading
down the line

Fig. 9b.
The same stroke
as the bowler sees it

Fig. 10.
The start of the off-drive:
the left shoulder has turned to lead
on to the intended line of the stroke:
the left hip has not been allowed
to fall away: the head, close to the
left shoulder, is looking down the
line of the ball

At the end of a well-hit drive, whether played with a single stride or with a *chassé*, the batsman should find himself with his weight firmly balanced on his front foot, with his head still leading, and knowing that the whole face of the bat was moving down the line of the ball at the moment of impact.

Power in driving comes from a combination of arm-swing, wrist-work and timed transference of weight: batsmen must be warned against 'pressing' which generally takes the form of the right hand and the right shoulder coming in too early and warping the true swing. They must realize that to drive well they must keep the arc of the swing true and smooth. To quote a maxim of one of the greatest of drivers, they must 'think speed not strength'.

In teaching the off-drive the coach will do well to stress the supreme importance of the left shoulder: **the wider the ball, the more should the batsman in the initial back-lift turn his back on the bowler** and the more, in fact, will the bat start its downward movement from the direction of fine

Fig. 11a.
The start of an on-drive:
the left shoulder has dipped
and the left foot has opened
to lead the line of balance
on to the line: the bat has
been pushed back by the
left arm towards first-slip

leg. Young batsmen should be warned that the quick-footed drive to the **wide** off-ball is a difficult stroke, involving as it does a movement not only down the pitch but outwards as well.

Most coaches will agree that young players find no stroke more difficult to master than the on-drive. Their great difficulty seems to lie in the transference of the line of balance to the on-side and the relative opening up of the left foot on which this depends (Figs. 11a and 11b). A coach may find that he can give them a clear idea of the initial movement required by telling them to imagine that they are moving to catch a full-pitch just in front and wide of their left knee. They will find that to do so they will slightly drop their left shoulder and that this will naturally lead the left foot to move out on the right line.

Very few boys under the age of fourteen or so have the strength and body control necessary to drive with any effect and security, but as soon as they can command these, the coach should regard it one of his chief duties and privileges to initiate and encourage them in this, the most satisfying of all cricket strokes.

Fig. 11b.
The finish of an on-drive:
the head has led the full
transference of weight on to
the front foot

Fig. 12.
The finish of an
off-drive:
the head, body, and
the straight left arm
have led right through
on the line of the
stroke: the wrists have
'broken' after the ball
has been hit

Fig. 13. The finish of an off-drive: in this case the full blade of the bat has been kept open in the follow-through; the left arm has only bent after the ball has been hit

The common faults in driving are:

(i) Not picking the bat well up.

(ii) Not getting the left foot out to and close up against the pitch of the ball.

(iii) Not leading with the head and left shoulder so as to bring the eyes and body balance on to the line of the ball.

(iv) Allowing the right hand to come into the stroke too early so that the arc is shortened and pulled across the line instead of being kept long, flat and smooth, with the bat face travelling down the line for as long as possible.

(v) Trying to hit too hard with consequent loss of body balance and movement of the head.

(vi) Not working the right foot up behind the left in the quick-footed drive: this is essential if the movement is to be kept smooth, the head steady and the left shoulder is to remain on the line.

V. T. Trumper. The start of a straight drive: a perfect example of a full back-lift and of how the head and shoulder lead.

Barry Richards. The perfect square-drive off the front foot. The ball has been played late, and with tremendous power.

88a

Wally Hammond. Finish of an off-drive: a wonderful study of balance and power

Len Hutton. Finish of an off-drive: the left leg has gone right out and over to the line of the ball

88b

THE BACK-STROKE IN DEFENCE

The hallmark of good back play is the use the batsman makes of the ground between the creases: the farther he moves back with his right foot, the longer he has to watch the ball and the easier it is to play it: he can thus, in fact, turn the length ball into one comfortably short of a length and the ball just short of a length into something like a long-hop which can then be dealt with offensively.

The second principle is that the right foot should move not only back but as far on to the line of the ball as possible, so that the bat, swinging straight, has just room to clear the right pad as it moves down that line.

Thirdly, the back, like the forward stroke, must be played sideways and controlled with the left arm and wrist: only so can the face of the bat be kept moving full down the line of the ball.

The mechanism of the stroke can now be analysed:

The feet

All good back players make full use of the ground between the creases and the coach must emphasize most strongly the importance of the initial movement of the right foot – well back and on to the line of the ball. The foot will land firmly and flat: in case of a straight ball the toe will be pointing more or less parallel with the crease; if the ball is outside the off stump and the back stroke aimed at mid-off or wider, the toe will be pointing backwards of the crease; conversely to a ball on, or just outside the leg stump and for a stroke aimed at mid-on or wider, the toe will point more towards cover.

The left foot follows the right, finishing in a position of natural balance close to it, with the heel released and the toe some inches in front of the right foot's instep and pointing to extra-cover.

The body and head

Though inevitably following the right foot as it moves back, it is most important that the body and head should keep their forward poise as much as possible (Fig. 14).

At the moment of impact, the line of balance on the braced right leg will be forward and into the stroke, with the head leading, immediately above the bat handle and directly behind the line of the ball.

The arms and hands

The left arm and wrist lead and control the stroke. At the moment of impact the left elbow will be high. Some batsmen find it natural to shift the grip of their left hand, sliding it round the handle until its back faces the wicket-keeper.

M.C.C.—7

The right hand will open into a thumb and finger grip: many batsmen in playing back defensively slide it down to within an inch or two of the blade.

The defensive back-stroke is played mainly with the hands and with comparatively little arm swing.

The bat

The bat will move with its full face down the line of the ball, with the hands slightly in advance of the blade at the moment of impact which should be made just in front of the right knee.

In a defensive back-stroke there will be no follow-through.

The chief faults to be expected here are:

(i) Not stepping far enough back with the right foot and not moving far enough over to get on to the line of the ball.

Fig. 14. The start of a back-stroke: the right foot has moved well back, parallel with the crease: the left shoulder, arm and hand are in full control

(ii) Not keeping the head and the balance of the body forward in playing the stroke.

(iii) Not keeping sideways to the line of the stroke.

(iv) Not making the left hand control the bat and keep its face on the line of the ball,

and not allowing the right hand to relax into a thumb and finger grip.

(v) Not keeping the left elbow up (Fig. 15).

THE BACK-STROKE IN ATTACK

The safest of all methods of forcing for runs a ball that is short of a length is by an attacking back-stroke played past the braced right leg.

To play this stroke effectively, the batsman must make the most of his height, even rising slightly on the toes of his right foot. He will find that

Fig. 15.
The back-stroke:
notice the high left
elbow, the relaxed
grip of the right hand
and the left heel just
eased

Fig. 16.
The finish of a forcing
back-stroke:
the batsman has made the most
of his height and the bat has
followed right through on the
line of the ball

he has got to give himself a little more 'room' than in the case of the defensive back-stroke.

The bat swing, as with the drive, will be lengthened and accelerated. The left arm will still control the arc of the stroke, but the right hand, still with a thumb and finger grip, will reinforce it with a punch just before impact.

In playing the stroke the elbows will be sharply bent: the body must be kept sideways: **the wider the ball is to the off, the more must the back of the left shoulder be turned on the bowler.**

The power comes largely by timing the transference of body weight into the stroke, and by the acceleration of the hands just before impact.

The face of the bat will be kept full on the line of the stroke for as long as possible, and on no account must the head and the line of balance be allowed to fall away (Fig. 16).

STROKES PLAYED WITH A HORIZONTAL BAT

Though the straight bat moving down the line of the ball is the basis of batting security, some of the most effective scoring strokes are those played with a relatively 'cross', i.e. horizontal, bat: moreover these strokes, in which the right hand dominates, are by far the more natural.

A too exclusive concentration on straight play may end by coaching these natural strokes out of the system, and the coach may well have the mortification of seeing his pupils playing with immaculate 'rectitude' but beaten by opponents in whom a good deal of 'the old Adam' survives.

After all, batsmen can only win matches by making runs, bowlers do not always bowl a length, and from balls of bad length runs are often most effectively, and can be quite safely, made by cross-bat strokes.

Most of all is this true of the full-pitch or the long-hop on or outside the batsman's pads, and **it has been well said that in most junior cricket the side that never bowled to leg and that hit every leg ball would never lose a match.** Yet how often, in fact, are they missed and will always be missed, unless the stroke is played right, and above all, unless the batsman gets and keeps his head on the line and really watches the ball.

The coach can offer young boys no earlier or more certain dividend in runs than by combining with the technique of straight bat defence that by which they can deal faithfully with the full-pitch or long-hop to leg: this may be analysed as follows:

HITTING THE LEG FULL-PITCH

The head

Once again, the head must lead the body in the stroke, moving forward and over on to the line of the ball: once there, with eyes looking straight

Fig. 17. Hitting a leg full-pitch: the head and left leg have led out on to the line: the ball will be hit at full stretch of the arms at, or in front of, square-leg

down the line of flight, it must be kept still and on no account be swayed over to the on-side with the impetus of the stroke.

The feet

The left foot will move forward and, if the ball is wide, outward on to its line: it will land pointing more or less down the pitch.

The body

The body will follow the lead of the head so that at the moment of impact its weight will be full on the left leg and its line of balance towards mid-on. The left knee must bend to allow the body to come through into the stroke (Fig. 17).

The bat

The stroke will be played with a strong arm swing, reinforced by the wrists. **The ball should be met at nearly the full stretch of the arms in front of the left leg: it cannot be properly hit if the elbows are kept tucked in.**

It is most important to get the bat out and on to the line of the ball quickly. The bat should hit the ball with a virtually full face: the straighter the ball, the more in front of square-leg should the stroke be aimed.

HITTING THE LEG LONG-HOP

The feet

As in back play, the first and vital move in the stroke is to take the right leg back towards the wicket: the farther and the earlier it moves, the longer the batsman has to watch the ball and the greater his command of it.

But whereas in the back-stroke the right foot will land facing point and just sufficiently inside the line of the ball to allow the bat face to move down it, with the body sideways to the stroke, it will now, in hitting the leg ball, move just to the off side of that line and the foot will point to extra-cover or even straighter, thus opening the body up square to the line of flight (Fig. 18a).

The left foot will follow the right back to a point level with, or a little in front of, the right, but well to the on side of it: the wider the ball is to leg, the farther will the left foot be carried away to the on side, i.e. the wider the gap between the right and left feet when set for the stroke, the object in every case being to get the head on to the line of the ball. Both knees will be slightly eased, to ensure that the weight is forward.

The body and head

The body, square to the line of flight, will lean well forward from the waist, with the head leading and the line of balance rather more on the left leg than on the right. **The forward poise of the body is most important. The head must be kept as still as possible.**

The bat

Both hands will maintain their full grip on the handle.

The bat, following the body turn in the backward movement that points the right foot to extra-cover, will automatically end its initial lift with its toe pointing to third-man. From there, wrists and arms in combination will whip it right forward and across the body, to meet the ball nearly at full arm stretch and more or less in front of the left leg.

In this movement the right hand will play the main part and the right wrist will tend to shut the face of the bat and so ensure that the ball is kept down (Fig. 18b).

Inevitably, as with the full-pitch, the wider the ball is to leg, the more behind square-leg will it naturally be hit. But the more the stroke can be aimed at, or even in front of, square-leg, the less chance there is of the batsman being late on the ball.

The main reasons why the leg ball, whether full-pitch or long-hop, is so often missed or ineffectively hit are:

(i) Not getting the head on to the line of the ball: and not looking at it.
(ii) Not freeing the elbows from the body so that the arms can get out to meet the ball.

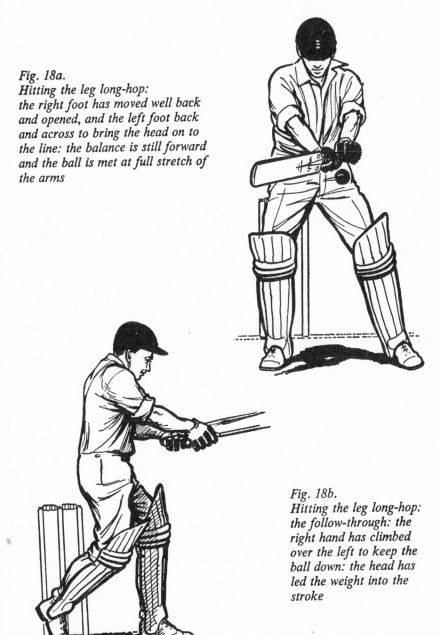

Fig. 18a.
Hitting the leg long-hop: the right foot has moved well back and opened, and the left foot back and across to bring the head on to the line: the balance is still forward and the ball is met at full stretch of the arms

Fig. 18b.
Hitting the leg long-hop: the follow-through: the right hand has climbed over the left to keep the ball down: the head has led the weight into the stroke

(iii) **Hitting late and aiming the stroke too fine.**

(iv) **Hitting too hard and thus swaying the body off balance and moving the head so that the ball is not truly focused.**

All that has been written above concerning the full-pitch and the long-hop is meant to apply only when the ball is well clear of the wicket on the leg side. The ball on the leg stump or on the inside of the batsman's pads should be forced past mid-on with a relatively straight bat.

THE HOOK

The term 'hook' is applied to the cross-bat stroke in which a short ball on the wicket, or even just to the off of it, is hit round to the on side.

To play it with safety, it is essential that the batsman should shift his right foot, and with it the line of his body balance, not only back, but far enough across to the off to be just outside the line of flight. In fact, he must by foot-work convert the ball into a long-hop to leg: once he has done so the mechanism for dealing with it is exactly the same as that which has been analysed above. But whereas he can be late for, or even miss, the long-hop to leg with impunity, this is not so with the hook played to the straight ball. He must be certain of hitting it, and, to be certain, he must be sure that he has plenty of time to watch it off the pitch.

On fast wickets, however short the ball, the hook is a dangerous stroke and must never be attempted until a batsman is well set: even then it demands quickness of eye, feet and wrist, if it is to be played successfully: even on easy paced or slow wickets the ball must be really short for the ordinary boy to be able to hook with any security. The easiest ball to hook is the long-hop that turns in from the off: leg-breaks are dangerous to hook.

In short, this stroke, though a profitable servant, is a most dangerous master, and the coach will be wise not to teach it at all in the early stages of instruction (Figs. 19a and 19b).

THE CUTS

The short off-ball can be dealt with in three ways, by the forcing back-stroke played with the straight bat as already described, by the cut played off the front foot, or by the normal cut played off the back foot.

Few really young batsmen can play the forcing back-stroke effectively, for it demands some stature or exceptional strength in their arms and hands. It is true that the cuts are played with a cross bat and therefore the margin of error is smaller, and to cut well and safely demands judgment of length, nicety of timing and flexibility of wrist: indeed the really gifted cutter is probably more born than made. But, just because it is played with a cross bat, it is to some extent a natural stroke, and most young batsmen of any ability can find in it a valuable weapon of attack, provided

Don Bradman. Finish of a quick-footed on-drive: this was the stroke which brought him the 100th run of his 100th century: balance and follow-through are perfect

Peter May. The finish of an on-drive: both arms have carried straight through in a long flat arc

96a

Colin Cowdrey. The defensive back-stroke just after impact: head right over bat, and bat and left elbow in one vertical line; right foot well back and parallel with crease

Colin Cowdrey. A forcing back-stroke: the left arm is in control; the full face of the bat has been kept open on the line of the ball

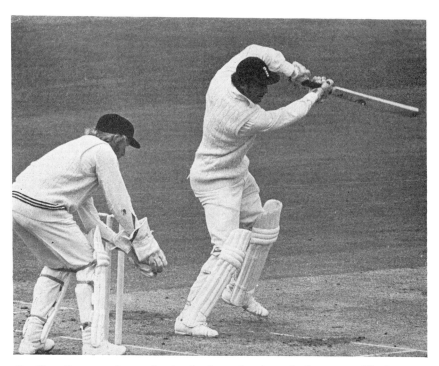

Geoffrey Boycott plays a forcing back-stroke through the covers. The batsman has taken his weight on the back foot, which is parallel to the crease. The poise of the body still remains forwards

Clive Lloyd. The finish of a hook stroke to a ball in line with the leg stump. The body has pivoted and the top hand has rolled over the bottom hand

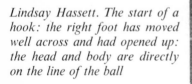

Lindsay Hassett. The start of a hook: the right foot has moved well across and had opened up: the head and body are directly on the line of the ball

Fig. 19a.
The start of the hook:
the right foot has gone right
back and points to mid-off:
the body is opening: the bat
has been lifted, mainly by
the right hand, towards
gully

Fig. 19b.
The finish of a hook:
the body has pivoted and
the right hand climbed
over the left to keep the
ball down

that they are helped to master its basic technique, and can learn to pick the right ball at which to play it and learn to watch the ball not only in the air but off the ground.

To play the stroke safely, it is essential that the batsman should be able to throw his arms and hands outwards and downwards on to the ball; it is therefore difficult to cut balls that are rising high, or that are near the wicket, and particularly dangerous to attempt the stroke to off-spin and in-swing bowling.

The majority of boys, however, with any natural batting ability will in fact try to cut, and the coach must try to help them to do so with as much effect and safety as possible, insisting above all on **the importance of coming down on the ball from above.**

THE CUT OFF THE FRONT FOOT

This is really a cross-batted hit, played to the really short and wide ball which is hit more or less at the top of its rise anywhere between extra-cover and square-third-man.

In as much as the batsman has to commit himself earlier, and to some extent gamble on the angle of rise, he has less margin of error than in the cut off the back foot, but if judgment and technique are right, it can be a stroke of great brilliance and power.

It is essentially a shot to be played on true wickets only, for the batsman has to commit himself to the stroke earlier than in the more normal cut off the back foot and to some extent has to gamble on the angle at which the ball will lift from the pitch.

The ball must be short and wide: the left foot will move well forward but not very far across to the off, for the batsman must have room to play it with a virtually horizontal bat which the wrists will throw at the ball at the full stretch of the arm, slightly shutting the face of the bat before impact (Fig. 20).

THE CUT OFF THE BACK FOOT

The stroke may be played comparatively early or late, with its line aimed relatively square or fine, but the mechanism is basically the same.

The feet

The movement of the right foot will depend on the line of the ball and the intended direction of the stroke. The right toe will point down the line of the intended stroke; the finer the cut the farther back will the right foot be taken. In both cases the left heel will be freed to allow full weight transference on to the right foot (Fig. 21).

Fig. 20.
Cut off the front foot:
just after impact: the ball has
been hit, with the bat face closing,
at full stretch of the arms and at
a point about parallel with the
left knee

Fig. 21.
A square-cut:
the arms and hands
have been 'thrown'
down and out into
the stroke with the
head leading the
weight over a bent
right knee

Fig. 22.
The finish of a late-cut:
the right toe points in the direction of the intended stroke and the batsman's back is almost turned on the bowler: the point of impact is almost level with the wicket

The head and body

These will follow the movement of the right foot. The head will lead the stroke in the direction in which the right foot is pointing, finishing over or even beyond the right foot: there will be a pronounced bend of the waist for the actual stroke and follow-through.

The bat

The proper back lift for the cut is most important and differs from the normal. The forearms and wrists moving round the body will extend the normal back lift upwards and backwards towards fine-leg so that at the top of the back lift the back of the bat is almost facing mid-on. The right elbow will be away from the side.

From there the arms and wrists will fling the bat outward and downward so that at the moment of impact the wrists are approximately above the right foot and the point of impact of the ball on the bat is appreciably behind it. The right wrist will turn the face of the bat over as it comes down from the stroke (Fig. 22).

The most common faults in cutting are:
(i) Not getting the bat up high enough to ensure that it comes down on to the ball from above.
(ii) Cutting too hard, which generally means jerking the head and so failing to focus the ball accurately, and dipping the right shoulder and so tending to get under the ball.
(iii) Meeting the ball too early: this tends to 'stun' the shot: the best cutters use the pace of the ball to help it on its way.

THE LEG GLANCE

Though the leg glance may be regarded as a refinement of batting, the ability to play it is a very real asset, provided always that the batsman recognizes that it is in no sense a substitute for, but only a variation of, the on-side strokes made with the full face of the bat. There is nothing to be said for 'tickling' a ball for one or two to fine-leg when it might safely be hit for four in front of or past square-leg.

The chief value of the leg glance is to be found on a fast pitch and against bowlers of some pace, especially when they are turning or 'running' the ball into the batsman. But with the fine-leg or leg-slip which such bowlers often position to counteract it, the stroke can be dangerous as well as profitable.

The leg glance is really a refinement of the forward- or the back-stroke and can be played, according to the length of the ball, off the front or back foot. In either case it is played with a virtually straight bat, but at the vital stage of the stroke the bat is moving rather across the line of the ball and the face of the bat is shutting. **There is therefore very little margin of error and the stroke should never be played to a straight ball.**

THE LEG GLANCE OFF THE FRONT FOOT

The most suitable ball for this stroke is one that is a good length and on, or only just outside, the batsman's pads. As with a forward stroke aimed at or just wide of mid-on, the head and left shoulder will lead the body out and over on to the line of the ball and the left wrist will keep the bat upright: but in the leg glide the left leg will be brought in its forward movement just inside the line of the ball, so that if it were missed it would hit the outside of the left pad. If the batsman is to have full command of the ball and be able to keep it down, it is most important that he should meet it only just in front of the left leg and almost directly under his head (Fig. 23). The angle of deflection will depend on the extent to which the bat face is shut at the moment of impact. With the margin of error necessarily smaller than in strokes played with the full face of the bat, it is all the more important that the ball should be watched with the utmost vigilance.

THE LEG GLANCE OFF THE BACK FOOT

This stroke is played most effectively to the ball just short of a length on, or just outside, the batsman's left leg: balls that are definitely short should not be glanced but forced in front of the wicket with the full face of the bat or hooked.

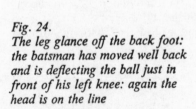

Fig. 23.
The leg glance off the front foot:
the ball has been met just in
front of, and outside, the left leg,
with the batsman's head right
on the line: the face of the blade
is just starting to close

Fig. 24.
The leg glance off the back foot:
the batsman has moved well back
and is deflecting the ball just in
front of his left knee: again the
head is on the line

As in the normal back-stroke, the right leg will be taken well back towards the stumps in order to give the batsman the maximum time in which to watch the ball: it must move sufficiently across the wicket to allow the left foot which follows it to position itself just inside the line of the ball: the right foot will be pointing to mid-off, the left approximately straight down the wicket. The head and line of balance at the moment of impact will be just in front of the left leg, and the ball will be met as near as possible to the left leg: **all the best exponents of the stroke let the ball come very close to them before they play it; indeed they seem to meet it almost under their noses** (Fig. 24).

The left hand will retain command of the bat until the last possible moment, when the right hand will co-operate in turning the bat face for the deflection.

RUNNING BETWEEN THE WICKETS

Efficient and well-judged running between the wickets is certain evidence of a well-coached and properly 'produced' school side. The standard in nearly all classes of school cricket is generally low, but will rapidly respond to tuition and practice. Boys should be made to realize that clear and sensible calling, quick running, and above all, quick turning are just as much parts of good batsmanship as proper stroke playing, and may easily mean an addition to their side's total that will determine the result of a match.

Such efficient running is often most unsettling to the fielding side which, unless well led and well disciplined, may easily be demoralized into mis-fielding and wild throwing with an expensive crop of overthrows. Moreover, the ability to call and run with safety quick, short singles from more or less defensive but steered strokes, can upset a bowler, who is thereby denied the chance of bowling to a plan over a series of balls to the same batsman.

Conversely, poor running not only loses runs but allows the field to be set deeper and so to cut off boundaries.

Finally, good running is enjoyable in itself – and especially to the spectators – reinforces the batsman's confidence and generally keeps the game alive.

The chief points to be taught are:

Calling

(i) Except when the ball goes behind the wicket, the striker must always call.

(ii) The call should be clear and decisive **YES** or **NO** or **WAIT**. Boys should be encouraged to make a habit of calling for every stroke.

(iii) For a hit that has passed the in-field and is obviously going some distance, the caller may, as he passes his partner, reinforce his first call of 'yes' with 'Probably two' or 'Probably three'; but this is merely a warning and must always be followed by a proper second call. The warning should not be given too loud, or the fielder concerned may overhear and accelerate.

(iv) For a second or subsequent run the call will always be made by the batsman who is running towards the wicket nearer to the fielder with, or in pursuit of, the ball.

(v) A call, if refused, must be refused at once with a decisive 'no': once the batsmen have really started to run, they must go straight through at all costs.

(vi) Running for 'mis-fields' is dangerous: there is a sound old saying 'never call for a mis-field unless there is a run and a half in it'.

Running

(i) The non-striker should stand well wide of the return crease: he should hold his bat in his left hand (his right, if the bowler is bowling round the wicket) and, as the bowler delivers the ball but not before, should move a yard or a yard and a half down the pitch. He must always remember that his partner's run is as important as his own.

(ii) In running, the batsman (whether striker or non-striker) must always be prepared to change his bat from left hand to right hand – or vice versa – to make sure that he can watch the ball and not have to look over his shoulder in turning. The striker should always try to run down that side of the wicket from which the bowler is bowling: but he may by force of habit find himself running down the off side when the bowler is bowling round the wicket, and if so it is the business of the non-striker to run well wide and outside him.

(iii) In 'making good his ground' each batsman should ground his bat at least two yards short of the crease and run it in along the ground. To dab the bat down at the end of the run is bad cricket and often leads to a run out.

(iv) Whenever there is any possibility, the batsman must always be looking for more than one run for a stroke. It is each man's job to complete the first run and turn as quickly as possible. Very many runs are lost, even in first-class cricket, by the tendency of batsmen to slow up over the last yard or two of their run-in, and half turn to see whether there may be another run or not. The right order is RUN, TURN, CALL.

Running practice

The coach should give his side occasional systematic practice out in the middle: this may at times be dovetailed into the fielding practice described in another chapter.

His team will bat in pairs, properly padded and gloved, for five minutes or so each: the bowling will, of course, be adjusted to the purpose of the

Don Bradman. Finish of a square-cut: the right arm has climbed over the left and the weight has gone into the stroke

Dennis Compton. Hitting a full-pitch to leg: the head has been brought on to the line of the ball and kept there. The ball was hit in front of square-leg at the full stretch of the arms

104b

practice; it need not be in overs but, as in match fielding practice, there should at some time be a switch from one end to the other in order to familiarize the field with the light and surface on each side of the pitch.

In this practice the coach should emphasize the importance of being always on the look out for the 'short single' from the stroke played slowly – indeed deliberately slowly – towards cover or extra-cover or to the left of mid-off and the right of mid-on: a stroke to either side of third-man offers a similar opportunity. In doing so, however, he will stress the relevance of the pace of the ground and the ability of the individual fielder. The call for a single for a ball played comparatively slowly to the left of cover may be perfectly sound if the ground is dead or if cover is slow, but suicidal on fast turf or if cover is a real specialist.

But whilst encouraging his boys to take every possible single and to turn ones into twos, and twos into threes, by quick turning and calling, the coach must realize that he is on dangerous ground, that run-stealing is heady wine, and that only experience can combine the art with security. **His last word must always be that a run is never worth the risk of a wicket.**

PLAYING AN INNINGS

Though the teaching of a sound technique may be the coach's chief pre-occupation, he will find that when it comes to match play, it must be reinforced by something else. It is one of the curious and fascinating things about cricket that a boy – or a man – may be far more or far less successful than his pure technique would seem to warrant, simply because he does, or does not, command the character and habit of mind that go to the playing of a long innings. One of the greatest of all English batsmen used to say 'Give me the batsman who makes runs: he is always in practice'. Every cricketer knows that a long innings in the middle is worth any number of nets.

Let us try then to get inside the mind of a young batsman and see how it can help him to play an innings. Let us suppose that he is number five in the batting order: the first wicket falls and he loses no time in getting padded up, for nothing is more unsettling than to have to do this under pressure and then hurry out to the wicket with his mind in a turmoil. Padded up now and with bat and gloves to hand, he can sit out in the sun, if there is any, to get accustomed to the light in which he will have to bat. He will watch the bowling carefully, trying to assess the particular problems that it may present, realizing perhaps that the medium-pace bowler at one end is coming off the pitch faster than his action would suggest, and that the slow bowler at the other, though giving the ball plenty of air, does not seem very easy to 'get at' on the half-volley. He will take good stock too of the placing of the field and its probable implications. Two slips and a gully, for instance, may suggest that a bowler is hoping to swing the ball away, two short-legs and a forward-mid-on that he is trying to swing it into the batsman.

Similarly he may conclude from what he sees that cover is a fine fielder with whom it would be dangerous to take a liberty, whereas there seems to be a safe run to third-man, who looks lethargic and who has to wind up to throw in, or to some fielder who is too deep.

Meanwhile, another wicket falls, and the returning batsman sits down beside him and begins to explain the rather obvious difficulty in which he has been at the wicket by an alarming picture of the bowling he has had to face. Our man will console himself with the reflection that, however difficult his friend may have found the bowling, No. 1 is still there and seems to have been meeting it in comparative comfort! He knows too that the wicket is often a little lively in the first hour before the dew is out of it, but that if he can be not out at lunch it will be easy enough afterwards.

But it is only a quarter to one when No. 4, exhilarated after a shaky start by at last timing an off-drive perfectly, runs for a hit that goes straight and fast to cover's left hand and pays the penalty: the score is 57 for 3.

There is a stupid but rather widespread convention that the next man in should wait for the returning batsman to reach the pavilion before he himself leaves: but our team's coach will have none of this, and with an 'in you go: watch the ball', speeds No. 5 on his way.

He walks out to the wicket, as a cricketer should, briskly but without hurry, and as he moves, he finds his mind repeating those last words of his coach 'watch the ball', and reminding himself that after all, whoever is bowling, **batting consists of playing one ball at a time and that in playing it nothing matters so much as really watching it.** He has time, too, to reflect that his side cannot afford to lose another wicket cheaply, that No. 1 is now well in and going strong so that the more that he gets of the bowling the better, and that his own job is undoubtedly to play himself in quietly and 'bat for lunch'.

He takes guard, has one last look at the field to fix it in his mind, and then settles down to face a quick bowler with a gentle wind from the leg-side. The first two balls are some six inches outside the off stump, and fairly well up: rather nervously he pushes forward at both, misses both, and hears second-slip gasp and the wicket-keeper mutter something under his breath. So far from being upset by this, he reflects that his luck must be in but that he would be unwise to tempt it further, and that for the next over or two he will do well to watch that type of ball go by.

An extra fast straight and shorter ball finds him very nearly late with his back-stroke, and he remembers that at the start of an innings it is as well against quick bowling to curtail the back-lift.

At the other end he sees his partner deal competently with an over from a slow left-hander and tucks away in his memory the fact that, though this man's stock ball spins away with the normal left-hander's break, the last ball of the over came in two or three inches off the ground with his arm – he must watch the ball all the way and not 'play at the bowler's arm'.

He has been in ten minutes and has still to make his first run, but this does not worry him at all, for what matters is not that he should 'break his duck', but that he should be still there and getting a sight of the ball.

Later on a glance at the score-board shows the total to have reached 95, his partner's score 47 and his own 13. No stupid superstition distracts him, for he reflects that it is the first 10 runs that take the most getting and that he has met and mastered the first attack: and how well his partner is playing, and how good it will be to see him get 50, especially as he has recently been out of luck and yet has never allowed it to get him down. What a satisfaction therefore it is when, by a quietly played push for a single off the first ball of the next over, he can give him the bowling and then by fast running and quick turning run three for a wide on-drive and see him safely home.

So to lunch, with the total raised to 108 and his own to 21. The cricket lunch of today does not offer the temptations to which our man's father might have fallen, with a resulting slowing up of his reactions, and soon after lunch he has his pads on again and is asking a friend to bowl him a ball or two, for he is taking no chances and this will get his eye and hands working together again.

As he goes out to bat, he reminds himself that no batsman can, after an interval, expect to go on exactly where he left off, but must play himself in again: in fact he must once again concentrate for all he is worth on watching the ball. Moreover three quarters of an hour's sun may have quickened the wicket a trifle and he must beware of being late to the fast bowler with whom they are sure to reopen the attack. He reflects too that, this being a one-day match, he must, if he is lucky enough to get going again, keep his eye on the clock and try to push on fast enough to give his captain a chance of a good declaration before tea.

For a time all goes well: 30 runs are added and a strong off-drive to the boundary and a firm and a perfectly timed push wide of mid-on for two have reinforced his confidence, when suddenly things begin to happen at the other end. His partner has been dealing faithfully with a slow leg-break bowler, meeting him quick-footed and driving him firmly along the ground into the long-field; but, forgetting the bowler's obvious answer, he tries the same stroke to a ball pitched much wider of the off stump and spinning away, and is stumped. In the same bowler's next over No. 6, a dangerous but rather a scatterbrained hitter, omits to notice where deep-square-leg is standing and hits a high full pitch, possibly bowled on purpose, straight down his throat. Next ball his successor, a pawky player, plays back to a length ball which he expects to break from leg, but which, coming through straight with top-spin, has him l.b.w.

The whole balance of the game has swung round. Instead of a comfortable 145 for 3, the board reads 157 for 6, and our man is uncomfortably aware of a decided tail of a wicket-keeper and two bowlers who cannot be relied upon for much: in fact the only real batsman left is now leaving the pavilion, a player of real promise, but young and, with his colours yet to earn, rather nervous.

He pushes tentatively forward at the two remaining balls of the slow bowler's over, misses them both, and is nearly stumped off the last. His partner is human enough to know what he is feeling, and cricketer enough to go down the wicket and say quietly to him, 'Don't worry: we'll pull this round together: this chap is coming off the wicket quite slowly and you can play him easily off the back leg, unless he is right up to you: just watch the ball'. This steadies the young player but the bowlers, elated by success, try for all they are worth to press home the attack and for several overs give nothing away.

Time is slipping by and runs are needed now if there is to be a real chance of a win. His partner cannot be expected to force the game, but he is a fine runner between the wickets, and our man reflects that two or three singles an over can push the score along: so he sets out to get them, now steering a back-stroke just wide of mid-on, now pushing a forward stroke wide of mid-off's left hand, now chopping a ball to third-man, still obligingly on his heels. These tactics unsettle both bowlers and fielders: there is a four over-throw and another wild return hits the fast bowler half-volley on the shin: this provokes him into letting fly two extra fast ones both of which are rank long-hops and are promptly hooked to the boundary, and our man is past his 50 without even having thought about it.

The applause that greets it is sweet music indeed, but he has still a job to do, for stumps are not drawn until seven and his side still need some 30 runs more to make the declaration they would like. It is up to him to stay and get them, for nothing loses time as much as losing wickets and in any case the remaining batsmen may not get them at all.

The fast-bowler has shot his bolt and has been replaced by the slow left-hander who, realizing that the wicket is not taking spin, is now concentrating on the ball that comes with his arm, with two short legs and a forward mid-on. Our man realizes that these are a serious threat to his young partner's forward push stroke: he determines to move them: after all, he will be hitting 'with the tide' and, if he looks at the ball and does not have a 'blind swipe', the truly hit on-drive that should follow will be an unpleasant business for the 'leg trap'. His tactics succeed: a swinging hit nearly decapitates mid-on who retires discreetly, whilst a second leads to the forward-short-leg being dropped back on to the boundary, thus opening the way for both batsmen to play the swinger quietly for ones and twos into the on-side gap.

So the runs come and the captain waves from the pavilion to call his batsmen in: and very happily they return, the younger knowing that he has helped to hold the fort and is sure of his place in at least the next two matches, the older feeling that he has gained valuable experience in an innings to which mind and character have contributed as much as technique.

5

Captaincy

Captaincy wins matches and can lose them, but it should do more than that; it can make or mar a season, not only in terms of wins or losses but in the general satisfaction and happiness which playing cricket should bring and which constitutes the real reason for playing it. Schoolboy captains can do a great deal not only for the elevens they lead but for the cricket of their school in general. For their term of office they receive in trust its cricket tradition.

The method of their selection or nomination varies in practice within wide limits, but there seems little to be said for the system whereby the senior colour surviving from the previous season automatically succeeds to office. Experience is certainly an asset; so is personal prowess; but neither is so important as character, personality and the capacity to think and learn about the game. **The sovereign virtue in a captain is unselfishness:** he must put others before himself.

Most boy captains have a senior adviser, amateur or professional – in some cases both – and they will be wise to avail themselves of their much greater experience and to welcome from them a post-mortem after each game and a 'staff talk' before the next one; sometimes the whole eleven will share in these, for much can be gained by illustrating tactical or technical principles from recent experience. Good captains are always learning.

A captain's administrative responsibility will vary very widely according to the nature of his command: it may be mainly concerned with individual matches or it may cover the whole organization of his school cricket. The wider it is, the more will he need the guidance and support of his coach and the wiser he will be to recognize that in seeking it he is in no real sense impairing his own authority or prestige. No boy captain can possibly anticipate all the demands that will be made on him, and the best are those that realize from the start how much they have to learn. Conversely, the coach will be most careful to avoid any appearance of dictation: his task is to anticipate the captain's problems, offer with tact suggestions for their solution, and progressively build up the captain's confidence both in the 'partnership' and in himself.

If he is to be a real leader, a captain must study his team as individuals, get to know their temperaments and how best to handle each one of them, not only on the field, but off it.

Discipline is essential in any cricket team, but the best discipline is not imposed but stems from a personal relationship in which confidence in and loyalty to the captain is automatic.

He must be an optimist and inspire optimism in his side: he must show confidence in them in order that they may feel confidence in him. By personality and example he can set and keep his team alight. He must try to cultivate and show equanimity: however desperate the situation, his team must never be allowed to sense that their captain is 'rattled'. **Encouragement is everything** – it may be for a bowler when things are going wrong with him, for a fielder who has missed a catch, or for a young batsman faced with a crisis or out of form.

Criticism should always be constructive: slackness and conceit alone merit and should get the rough side of the captain's tongue, and even then it is generally better to give it off the field than 'in the middle'.

A captain – or his secretary, and even then the ultimate responsibility is the captain's – must think ahead and answer letters promptly. Staff work must be precise and not improvised to meet the unforeseen. A captain must know the Laws of Cricket and the 'Notes' that accompany them; this means some quite hard work. Very few players really know the Laws.

In all home matches he must, whenever possible, be on the ground to greet his opponents on their arrival and see them off at the end of the day. He must make sure, before the game starts, that his opposite number is familiar with, and agreeable to, the 'custom of the ground' in such matters as hours of play, intervals and boundaries.

He will remember that he is a host and will do all that he can to entertain the visiting side; he will impress this too on his own team and ensure that at luncheon and tea they split up and look after their guests' needs before their own.

Umpires and scorers will not fail to appreciate a word of thanks at the end of a match.

He must insist on punctuality: his side should be ready to take the field at least five minutes before the umpires go out: his batsmen must be 'padded up' in good time, and he should ensure that the ingoing batsman passes the outcomer on the field of play.

He should insist on his eleven turning out tidily and, so far as it is possible, in 'uniform': the cricket field is not the place for idiosyncracy in dress. Periodic boot inspections are advisable: neglect may lose a match.

He should see that his bowlers, especially his openers, 'loosen up' before they take the field.

IN THE FIELD

A captain should aim at so training his team that he becomes automatically a focus for their attention in the field. It should never be necessary for him to attract any fielder's attention by calling out his name or to 'semaphore' for a change of position. If they are properly trained, they will always have an eye on their leader and respond to unobtrusive signals. He himself will form the habit of looking round his field at the start of every over to make sure that it is placed as he wishes. He must insist on accurate positioning but he must beware of being over-fussy with small and often quite meaningless adjustments. **He must, before he takes the field, have a clear idea in his head of his general tactical plan.** He must know how he wants to dispose his field for each of his bowlers, but should be prepared to listen to their views, though not necessarily take them. He should also have thought out what adjustments will be necessary for each if a left-handed batsman comes in: many boy captains are apt to get into a serious tangle when faced with this problem.

In general he will place his field for each bowler as he hopes he will, not as he fears he may, bowl. He must realize that, the faster the ground, the deeper a fieldsman can stand and still save 'one'; the converse is equally true. He must avoid 'half-way places', too deep to save one and not deep enough to cut off the fours.

He will always try to keep as many of his fielders as possible in their 'specialist' places, but he will never allow any of his team to regard themselves as specialists pure and simple; they must all be prepared to field anywhere, though the slip fielders should be as constant as possible, and he must not have his stock bowlers running and tearing themselves to pieces in the out-field.

He must keep his mind and his field elastic between attack and defence: this means watching the score, the clock and the individual batsman: with experience he will learn to assess one batsman as probably a back player, hooker and cutter, another as a driver, whether by the air or the land routes.

He will always attack a new batsman, bringing in his field to save singles and perhaps stationing a silly-mid-off or silly-mid-on to unsettle him: he will encourage his bowlers to bowl straight.

There are times when he will be attacking one batsman and defending against the other, even perhaps to the extent of giving the latter singles by opening out his field in order to get him away from the bowling.

In general, the better the pitch and the more set the batsman appear to be, the more must a captain be prepared to experiment, especially with his slow bowlers, even at the cost of runs. If the batsmen really threaten to get on top, he must tell his bowlers to bowl outside the off stump and support them with a two-ring field, the outer ring to save the fours. The more difficult the pitch the more he must rely on his best length bowlers and set his field 'tight' to pin the batsman down: if he has a good left-hander, this is above all time to use him. He should read the tactical sections in the bowling chapters of this book and study the field diagrams in them.

At all costs he must try to retain the initiative and dictate to the batsmen and not be dictated to. If he feels that this initiative is slipping from him, any move is better than no move: to change a bowler's end is often as good as a change of bowling: he must never let the game 'run on'.

He will never allow irresponsible appeals from fielders who are not in a position to see: 'Collective appealing' should be anathema. On the other hand bowlers and wicket-keepers should, if necessary, be reminded that 'them that asks nought, gets nought', and that the umpires are there to give a verdict.

MANAGEMENT OF BOWLING

To make the best use of his bowling resources is the captain's most important and difficult task. A weak bowling side has to live by its wits – which means its captain's. He must first of all know his bowler's capabilities and temperaments and be able to handle them in the right way: much can be done by friendly discussion off the field to increase a bowler's grasp of tactics and to build up the morale necessary for what is always an arduous and at times a discouraging job: much, too, can be done on the field by suggestion and encouragement or a steadying word, and this is always easier if the captain is in close contact with the bowler, e.g. at mid-off. Such personal knowledge of his bowlers will often help a captain to sense after an over or two that X is 'feeling like it today' or that there is something wrong with Y's delivery timing, that his confidence is shaken, and that it will be unwise to experiment with him for long.

But there will be much besides the personal equation of his bowlers to occupy the captain's mind. His bowling policy may sometimes be dictated – or at least influenced – by the direction of the wind and often by the state of the pitch which may vary from hour to hour and at times between one end and the other: for length is relative to the pace of the pitch, as well as to the pace of the bowler, and the captain will not hesitate if necessary to urge his bowlers to raise or lower their length target. All the time he will be watching the individual batsmen at the wicket and trying to adjust his attack to them: for instance, the firm-footed or the nervy batsman may invite a slow bowler, the impatient dasher may be soon driven to suicide by sheer length, the 'flincher', if he so reveals himself, will be made to face up to pace.

In general it is true that slow bowlers are a bad bet on dead pitches against batsmen of sense and experience, though many school batsmen are apt to get themselves into trouble with any bowler who will 'give the ball enough air'. **On sticky pitches accuracy is everything:** fours count and it is no time for experimentalists. Most tail-end batsmen are vulnerable to pace.

But perhaps the most difficult bowling equation a captain has to solve is between runs, wickets and time. Only experience can really help him to judge how long he can gamble for wickets with a spin bowler against a diminishing balance of runs and minutes: sometimes indeed whether he can risk at all the over or two which his spinner may need to find a length: whether his end-holder is really pinning a batsman down or merely playing him in: how long to keep his pace bowlers on at a stretch, especially if the weather is hot and it is a two-day match, bearing in mind both their physique and temperament and the natural rhythm of their action or lack of it. Success is a rare stimulant, and a bowler who feels himself on top does not readily feel tired, but a captain must beware of letting him run on into that extra over or two that may make a later comeback so much more difficult.

Of course his tactics will be dictated by the resources at his disposal. If he has a fast bowler of any merit, he will certainly open with him, but he must be nursed so that he can be brought on again to attack new batsmen and especially the tail. At the other end he will probably open with the bowler who is likely to make the best use of the new ball. The fast bowler should bowl down wind, if there is any, and the other man into it to help his swerve. But if this opening attack does not seem to be causing much difficulty, the captain may well experiment by switching them to opposite ends.

If he has not two bowlers who can use a new ball with effect, he must not be a slave to convention and may well try a contrast in pace and style, opening, for instance, with a swinger or fast bowler at one end and an off-spinner or slow left-hander at the other.

Leg-break bowlers, if only they will keep the ball up and if they are supported by good fielding and wicket-keeping, are of immense value in school cricket; indeed, a school team without one is only half armed. It is always worth trying them against any batsman who looks like getting set, and a captain should soon be able to judge whether he knows the answer or no. But such bowlers are apt to be expensive, especially on slow wickets, and it is generally important that the other end should be held as tight as possible with accuracy of length and direction.

The virtual disappearance of the lob-bowler is one of the regrettable mysteries of modern cricket: by virtue of his very novelty and its psychological effect even a moderate lob-bowler can be an asset to a school side: boys seem to think today that there is something *infra dig* in bowling under-hand, forgetting – or more probably never having heard – what some great lob-bowlers have achieved even in this century in the highest-class cricket. Given good spinning fingers, the ability to field well to his own bowling, determination and constant practice, it is not difficult for any boy with cricket sense to become at least an adequate lob-bowler, and a school captain should see whether one of his side cannot be trained to fill that role: indeed he might fill it himself and be surprised at the dividend.

A not uncommon mistake by school captains is to run through all their possible change bowlers before reverting to their first choices: they must balance in their minds the need for adequate spells of rest against what is tactically the best attack against any given batsman or in face of any given problem of runs and time. Similarly, though they must, of course, play every match as a match, they must think ahead through the season: a season's programme can be a heavy strain on young bowlers and it may sometimes be both wise and possible to take advantage of a weakness in the opposition to rest the stock bowlers as much as possible and seize the chance of giving their understudies a run and perhaps the valuable encouragement of some wickets.

THE BATTING ORDER AND DECLARATIONS

A captain should try to settle the batting order as early as possible in the season and to stick to it. Constant changes are unsettling, and generally a confession of weakness in the captain and in the side.

The opening pair are to some extent specialists: their first job is to weather the new ball and, to do so, experience of it as well as the right technique and the right temperament are important. But two purely defensive batsmen are not an ideal opening combination; it must never be forgotten that it is the aim of the batting side to wrest the initiative as early as possible from the bowlers, and to this end one of the openers at least should be potentially aggressive in temper and stroke play.

A left-hander may be of particular value at the start of an innings: school bowlers generally bowl less accurately to them, and the normally dangerous swerve with the new ball which leaves the right-hander is much less of a threat to a left-hander.

Numbers three and four may well be the two best batsmen in the side, ready, of course, if necessary, to hold the fort but with the strokes and the instinct of aggression to get on top and stay there: again, if one of them is a left-hander the side is lucky.

Of numbers five, six and seven, one should be a sheet-anchor, capable of redeeming an ugly situation by soundness of method and tenacity; the other two, we may hope, will be attackers ready to exploit a good start and to push the score along ahead of the clock.

The rest of the batting order will probably be predetermined for the captain in the shape of three bowlers and his wicket-keeper.

The captain should sit with his team for as much of their innings as possible; through his own experience and by closely watching the play he may often be able to help them, though he must never fuss them: they must feel that he is 'on the bridge' almost as much as when they are in the field. A word from him may do much to encourage a diffident or nervous batsman or to steady an excitable one. No batsman was ever the worse for being told, as he went out to bat, to look at the ball. It is for the captain to tell his batsmen, according to the state of the match, when he wants

them to try to force the pace and when to 'dig in'; they must never be left
in doubt as to what his policy is. The fall of a wicket often provides a
chance of conveying that policy to the batsman in the middle through the
man who goes out to join him. But as a rule the more the batsmen can be
left to play their natural game the better, though when the wicket is really
difficult and bowling on top, it is likely that brave hitting will pay better
than orthodox defence.

A great deal of nonsense is talked and written about declarations and the
response to them. It is the business of every captain to try to win a match
but, if he cannot do so, not to lose it. By all means let him err on the side of
taking a chance in the pursuit of victory, but so-called 'sporting declarations', which in fact give the side that bats second a good chance of winning,
and the side that declares little or none of bowling them out in the time
available, are not true cricket. The reasonable ratio of time to runs in a
declaration diminishes with the increase of the target to be reached.
Seventy-five minutes may be a fair allowance against a total of 120 whilst
two hours and a quarter may be reasonable for 180. The longer the journey,
the better chance the bowlers have and the less likely that a fast pace of
scoring can be consistently maintained. But the time ratio will also depend
on the state of the wicket, the pace of the outfield and the captain's knowledge of his own bowling and the other team's batting resources. In
pursuing a declared total he will rarely be wise to alter his order and put
his hitters in first, or even to instruct his openers to 'get on with it' at once.
The fall of early wickets in the premature pursuit of runs encourages the
bowlers and at the same time makes the continuance of that pursuit bring
the risk of losing the match. A good start is everything, even if for a time
the score falls behind the clock: with wickets 'in the bank' the later batsmen can accelerate with a greater confidence or, if need be, shut the door
to avoid defeat. It is for the captain to tell them which they are to do

It is in this second stage of the innings that the captain may be justified
in altering his order, bringing up his numbers six and seven, if they are
hitters, to replace a normally more stolid four and five, or holding back
his left-hander because he may cause loss of time.

He will be wise, too, to remind his batsmen that they must be out to take
every run they can by good running between the wickets: this in itself will
tend to unsettle bowlers and fielders and few boys realize that four singles
an over mean well over eighty runs an hour.

6

Learning by Watching

Though two of Wordsworth's nephews were the originators of the University cricket match, there is no reason to suppose that the poet had any interest in the game: yet he might well have had cricket in mind when he wrote the line 'as if his whole vocation was endless imitation'. For whatever may be done by precept in the teaching of cricket, the coach will be wise to give his young players every possible opportunity of watching the first-class game, for they will instinctively and more readily imitate what they see than interpret, remember, and reproduce what they hear or read.

Let us then imagine him with a party of enthusiasts setting out for such a day's watching. Before he starts, or perhaps on the way, he will try to impress on them how much they can learn if they will only use their eyes, their imaginations, and later on their memories. He may well attempt a sketch of the leading players who will be on view and the particular excellencies which are to be looked for in each, recalling, if he can, some of their great achievements in order to instil a proper sense of respect and emulation.

If they can arrive on the ground early, the party may well have a chance of a 'close-up' of some of the players at the nets, and the coach a first-rate opportunity of a running commentary on technique. Then there is the problem of where to sit: on the whole he will probably be right to aim for a place at one end of the ground, just to the off side of the bowler: this will give the party the best view of what the ball is doing, in the air and off the ground, and of the batsman's method, especially of that all important aspect of batting, the breadth and uprightness of the bat down the path of the ball. But if he and his party have to content themselves with a sideways view, they can console themselves with the thought that from here they can judge, much better than from end on, the pace of the ball through the air and off the ground, its length, and in case of slow bowlers, its flight. It was an education to watch Grimmett's 'dip' from a position square to the wicket. From here, too, it is possible to appreciate to the full how far really good batsmen move their feet in the back and forward strokes and how fast and how 'tidily' they move their feet for the quick-footed drive.

Having taken their places, wherever they may be, the party waits anxiously for the umpires, whose appearance may give the coach a chance to emphasize the vital importance of knowledgeable and attentive umpiring and to suggest that they should not take the umpires for granted but watch them too and the signals they give.

Now comes the fielding side, looking, let us hope, like a proper team, well-turned out, with clean boots and flannels, following close after their captain and obviously intent on business.

The placing of the field

The running commentary of the coach must, of course, be largely dictated by the incidents of the play, but he may well try to concentrate at times on certain general aspects of technique, in the hope that these may sink in and become part of his pupils' instinctive outlook on, and interest in, the game.

He may first comment on the distribution of the field in relation both to the particular bowler and batsman concerned, and the presumed state of the wicket, no doubt calling attention to the way in which the field automatically sorts itself out at the start of the match with little appearance of direction from the captain.

His commentary may well be prefaced by a series of questions, designed to make his listeners use their eyes and think for themselves, for instance:

(i) From the distribution of the field what do you think is the bowlers' general plan of attack?

e.g. (a) how can bowler A, opening with the new ball, justify having two slips and a gully and three men close in on the leg side?

(b) why for bowler B, a leg-spinner, do slip and gully stand unusually wide, and why is there that large gap in the outfield between straight-long-on and square-leg?

(c) why does bowler C, a slow-medium off-spinner, have no third-man, and why are his cover and mid-off so much straighter than for the leg-spinner?

(ii) What alterations in field distribution are made between Batsman A and Batsman B and why? Why towards the end of the innings, when a new batsman joins a colleague, not out 80, is the field so often adjusted for the last two balls of an over?

(iii) Why are mid-off, mid-on, extra-cover and cover, appreciably nearer in (or it may be further out) than when we watched a fortnight ago?

(iv) Why did forward square-leg chase that ball instead of mid-on who was really nearer to its line?

The technique of fielding

Next, concentrating on technique, the coach may emphasize some of the following points:

(i) The obvious and unremitting concentration of the slips and the close in leg fields: their stillness and balance as the ball is bowled, with their weight forward on the front part of their feet.

(ii) The inward movement towards the batsmen of all the other fields as the ball is bowled.

(iii) The position of the fieldsman's head, body, hands and feet, both in attack and in defence.

(iv) The pace at which the ball is chased or at which the outfield comes in to 'save two'.

(v) The balance for and speed of the throw-in: its length – always full-pitch, or long-hop to the wicket-keeper, or if to the bowler, the relay system so that he receives a quiet catch and is never made to stoop.

(vi) The way in which, if there is a chance of a run-out at the bowler's end, mid-off or mid-on will get up to the wicket to take the return and to save the bowler's hands.

(vii) The automatic backing up for the throw-in, with the backer-up always well away from the wicket.

Other general reflections might well be:

(i) The way in which a well-disciplined side will always keep their eyes on their captain who will never need to shout at them to secure their attention.

(ii) The ability of such a side to stick to it and keep its 'edge' even when it has been in the field for several hours and the score is 300 for 4.

(iii) The obvious enjoyment that good fieldsmen get out of the game.

(iv) The number of runs that good fielding can save in any given hour's cricket, and the reinforcement it provides to the bowler and the curb and frustration it presents to the batsman.

(v) The close attacking field (a) at the start of an innings, (b) when the bowlers are on top, (c) when time is short and the saving of runs not important.

Lessons from bowling

Switching his angle to the bowler and his craft, the coach may seek to drive home some of the following general ideas:

(i) The absolute regularity of the bowler's run-up, the rhythm of his delivery and his follow-through.

(ii) The use of the full width of the crease for altering the angle of attack.

(iii) The way that all good bowlers make the batsman play at the new ball by bowling straight and keeping it well up: the way they attack each new batsman.

(iv) Their skill in shutting up an end by bowling to their field: for this, control of direction, as well as of length, is vital.

(v) The use that slow and slow-medium bowlers make of 'flight' (best seen from square-on) and their readiness to be driven, in the expectation that artifice of 'flight' and width may induce a mistake.

(vi) The slight variations of pace by medium bowlers and the use by the fast bowler of an occasional 'yorker' and (or) extra-fast ball.

Above all let the coach drive home the principle that to be driven is never dishonour, to be hooked is ignominy, and that every ball which is played easily off the back foot is a mark against the bowler.

Lessons from batting

The following are some of the aspects of batting which careful watching may reveal and which the coach may do well to underline:

(i) The ease, balance and stillness of the batsman's stance.

(ii) The straight pick up of the bat, and the opening of its face to point.

(iii) The use of the feet: i.e. how far the good batsman moves his back foot to play back, and his front foot to play forward: how quickly and smoothly he moves out to drive, with the footwork never disturbing the sideways poise and balance of the body.

(iv) The way in which the head leads the feet and determines the player's balance.

(v) The way the left shoulder, arm and wrist control the arc of every straight-bat stroke.

(vi) The position of the left shoulder and hip: the wider the ball to the off, the more does the batsman in the initial movement turn his back on the bowler.

(vii) The length of time for which the face of the bat moves down the line of the ball.

(viii) The way the ball on the leg stump or inside of the pads is played straight-batted, and 'down the line', with the head and left wrist leading, and not hit right-handed and square.

(ix) The balance which is preserved in every stroke, even in hitting a rank long-hop or full-pitch to the boundary. Good batsmen never over-hit to the point of losing balance and so moving their heads.

There are, of course, many other points of interest of a less purely technical nature to rub in:

(i) The way a new batsman will play himself in quietly until he has sized up the nature of the attack and of the pitch: he will not be seen playing defensive strokes at length balls outside the off stump: he will watch them go by.

(ii) The self-control and tenacity which refuse to be seduced by a couple of fine boundaries into taking a liberty with the next ball, and which regard the reaching of fifty not as an ultimate achievement, but rather as encouraging evidence that a long innings is on its way.

(iii) The readiness to play to the score or to the captain's orders without regard to personal average or interest.

(iv) The refusal to be 'rattled' when the bowlers are clearly on top and the batsman is, for the time being, clearly in difficulties.

(v) The way in which one batsman who is well in will, if need be, nurse a new and less confident partner.

But from no aspect of batting can the young watcher be more sure of learning a valuable lesson than from the running between the wickets. He should be encouraged to notice:

(i) The way the non-striker backs up.

(ii) The quickness and decision of the calling.

(iii) The way the bat is run-in along the ground at the full stretch of the arm.

(iv) The importance of completing the run and the turn as quickly as possible before the call for the second or third run is made.

(v) The ease with which short singles can often be run, provided that both batsmen know and trust each other and that call and response are made at once.

7

Net Practice

However true it may be that boys can best be initiated into and reminded of the basic techniques of batting and bowling by explanation, demonstration and the practices analysed in the Group Coaching chapter that follows, **the fact remains that fundamentally cricket is single combat – a bowler bowling and a batsman playing a single delivery. This is the essence of match play and the end of all practice is to train the player not only in the physical technique but in the judgment, considered and instinctive, that he will need in a match.** The most immaculate forward stroke may be futile and even fatal if played to the wrong ball or if not properly timed: a couple of perfectly executed off drives may be a snare and a delusion if they lure the batsman into trying to execute another to an apparently similar but in fact slightly different ball.

It is important, then, that in all practice the essentials of match play should never be lost sight of: it must train the mind and the will as well as the body. How to do this, in general and still more in relation to the individual with his special factors of physique and temperament, is perhaps the greatest problem in coaching, for on the coach will depend the creation and maintenance of this atmosphere throughout a net.

The lay-out

Too much trouble cannot be taken to provide the best possible net pitches. Indeed their condition is even more important than that of the match ground, for on bad pitches batsmen cannot learn a correct method nor build up the confidence on which much of it depends, while bowlers are flattered by them and may get a rude awakening when they find themselves at work on a pitch that gives them no help.

Boys should be made to realize very clearly that they must themselves be prepared to do all they can to make their nets as good as possible. They should expect to have to roll the pitch before and after each practice: indeed if the ground is being cut up, it pays to run a roller over it once or twice between each batsman's innings. If the pitch consists of matting or any other such cover, care must be taken to see that it is properly stretched and pegged down. The bowling and return creases should be clearly marked, for unless this is done, bowlers may easily get into the habit of bowling no-balls. The coach will periodically inspect the netting to make sure that any holes are properly patched, for these can be really dangerous.

All cricket gear, pads, gloves, etc., should be kept behind, or well to the side of the net. If there is no clock visible, the coach should be sure to have a watch to ensure the accurate timing of relays.

The ideal number for a net is probably three, certainly never more than four, excluding the coach who should be free to talk and (or) bowl as he thinks fit from time to time. Often, of course, he will have to divide his attention between several nets; he must harden his heart against the very real and natural temptation to bowl at and commend the boy who is doing well, to the neglect of the boy who probably needs his help much more, but is for the moment showing discouragingly few signs of profiting by it.

Net discipline

Before we go further, let us consider for a moment the need for what we may call 'net discipline'. Haphazard slip-shod net practice may well do more harm than good. Boys must be made to realize that, to make the best of a net, they must try for all they are worth, both for their own sake and for the sake of those who share it with them. Most boys, when their turn comes to bat, will wish to make the best of their batting time, though many have but little idea how to do so, but the bowling only too often will, after a serious enough start, degenerate into mere slinging or wild experimentation to the detriment of the bowler himself and the frustration of the batsman.

Bowlers must take their proper run and be very careful not to bowl too soon after each other: the batsman must be given time to settle down properly before each ball. Batsmen, for their part, must be scrupulous to return the balls they pick up from the back and the near sides of the net by throwing easy catches to the bowlers; they should never make them stoop by knocking the balls back along the ground with their bats.

The order of batting, if not posted by the captain on the net list, should be laid down clearly by him or the coach before a net starts. It is the coach's job to warn the next man to 'pad up' a minute or two before his predecessor is due to end his innings: such padding up should, of course, always be carried out behind the nets.

Whether batsman or bowler, any boy who, after a friendly word of warning, is clearly making no effort to do his best for himself or the others at his net, should be told that his room is better than his company.

Conduct of a net

Most coaches find it far more difficult to give real help to bowlers at a net than to batsmen and, as a result, it is certainly the case that the latter get more attention than the former. But the good coach will never let his bowlers feel that they are being taken for granted as mere adjuncts to net practice: he will be constantly watching their run-up, action and follow-through, stressing the importance of concentration, testing and challenging their accuracy by demands for, e.g. four successive balls just over a length and just outside the off stump, and stimulating their tactical sense by asking how, on observation of a given batsman's methods, they would propose to attack him in a match.

He will, of course, also be on the watch to see that a bowler does not get overtired and, if he detects this, will not hesitate to tell him to have a rest or pack up altogether. This indeed is one of the greatest problems of net practice – and increasingly so as the season advances – to provide the batsmen with the best possible opposition and at the same time ensure that the bowlers are not over-worked: for bowlers get stale far more readily than batsmen, and they are the rarer and more precious cricket commodity.

But we must assume for the purpose of our study of the conduct of a net that it is early in the season, that all the players are fit and fresh, and that the coach, however awake he may be to the needs of his bowlers, is on this occasion primarily concerned with the batsmen.

The duration of each batsman's innings may, of course, depend on the time available for the net as a whole: much can be done in ten minutes; few boys can bat profitably at a net for more than twenty, for it is, or should be, really hard work, and by the end of that time it is likely that, even if they are not beginning to tire physically, their concentration is on the ebb. So we will compromise with a fifteen minute spell.

Before his innings starts the batsman should be given an approximate picture of each bowler's field, e.g. where a leg-break bowler has stationed his deep-fields, whether an off-spinner has two or three close-short-legs, and so on.

At the start of his net innings the batsman should play exactly as he would when he first goes in during a match, i.e. concentrate on playing himself in, getting the pace of the pitch and sizing up the bowlers opposed to him. He should, of course, not be discouraged from making strokes in his opening spell when the right ball comes along, but he must be brought to realize that a long-hop before he is sure of the pace of the pitch, or an apparent half-volley before he has mastered the bowler's flight, may not be the gift which they appear and which indeed they may well prove to be when he is fully 'in'.

During this initial phase the bowlers will be urged to attack for all they are worth and be firmly reminded that it is criminal not to make the batsman play each ball, especially if it is swinging: that they must keep the ball up, and that every ball they bowl to which he can play back without hurrying is 'one up' to him and 'one down' to them.

For the second and middle phase of the innings the coach may well concentrate on improving the production of one or more particular strokes, particularly the forcing strokes which the batsman may not yet have the

confidence to play in a match. Above all he should encourage any boy who, he thinks, can do so to drive, really drive, the over-pitched ball: the moment when a boy batsman first feels the thrill of a truly timed drive which sends a half-volley skimming over mid-off's head is a milestone in his cricket life. The bowlers may well be asked to co-operate in providing the raw material that the batsman needs: it will do them no harm if for an over or so each they concentrate on trying to bowl a series of half-volleys to order, straight or wide as is required: but when it comes to long-hops and full-pitches to practise hooking or hitting to leg, it may be better for them not to bowl at all but to throw.

The coach may sometimes find it effective to collect all the net balls and bowl or throw the type of delivery he wants at a shortened range, even from half-way down the pitch. This should ensure accuracy and certainly mean a real saving of time.

For the last third of the innings there is nothing so stimulating as an imaginary match. The coach, summing up the relative abilities of the batsman and the attack opposed to him, will lay down a 'match target' of so many runs: the bowlers will declare their field and the two parties will then tackle each other in deadly earnest. It will be for the coach to determine the runs in any given stroke and whether or no a possible chance was taken: he will be lucky – or perhaps unlucky – if he does not find himself the target for heated remonstrance at times from bowlers and batsmen alike, for it is wonderful how stimulating such a contest can prove to be, even at the end of a long and hot net, and how it can satisfy the most normal and imperative of every young cricketer's instincts, that 'cricket should be fun'.

8

Group Coaching—Why and How

It seems a fair assumption that those who really know anything about cricket – and about boys – will agree that it is a game worth playing, not only for the enjoyment it gives and for the friends it makes, but for the training it can and should provide for body, mind and character, and for the contribution which that training can make to happiness and good citizenship.

They will probably also agree that most small boys, given any opportunity, start by being eager to play it, but that all too few retain that early enthusiasm in face of the discouraging conditions with which they have to contend.

The root of their discouragement lies in the deplorable lack of playing facilities and of elementary coaching in the basic 'skills' of the game. To a great extent these two factors run together, for, unless the practice pitches are reasonably true it is impossible to coach effectively, and on bad pitches the young batsman may well fail to profit by such coaching as he has had, whilst the bowler is flattered into thinking that he can dispense with it. A boy who is always out almost as soon as he is in will not long continue to play cricket.

All too few schools can command the resources to maintain turf pitches, whether match or practice, which will stand up to the wear and tear of a season's play. For the great majority the answer, especially for practice, would seem to lie in the artificial pitch. There is no need for the coach to be afraid that boys trained on such a surface will be at sea when they come to play on turf. There is, of course, a great difference between, for example, batting on concrete and a soft grass pitch, and a certain adjustment of technique and timing there must be, which only experience can give: but the fundamentals learned under favourable conditions will still hold good: indeed there is and can be no substitute for them and they alone can ensure the success in terms of runs and wickets which will sustain a boy's enthusiasm for the game and keep him playing it.

There still remains the problem of how these basic principles of the game can be taught at an early stage to all who are anxious to learn them. Of course, there is no substitute for individual coaching at a net and it is a very natural temptation for the coach to concentrate on the few boys most likely to profit by it. But he will be doing cricket a greater service and in the

126

long run will reap a richer reward in the success of his teams, if he can, in the earlier stages, spread his coaching to cover all who want to play the game, and it is to meet this need that the technique of Group Coaching was evolved.

It is a matter of history that when, at the first conference on the M.C.C. Coaching Scheme, the idea of Group Coaching was first presented to the distinguished company of Test and County cricketers who attended, it was initially received with scepticism that bordered on incredulity. 'Teaching cricket by numbers', 'turning out robots', 'putting them all through a sausage machine': such were some of the terms of its early criticisms: but the proof of the pudding has been in the eating and today it is not only recognized as the only means by which the basic techniques can possibly be taught to all boys who wish to learn them in the conditions only too often still prevailing in many of our schools, but that it can also be of high value as a background and reinforcement of individual coaching, not merely for beginners, but for any young, or even not so young cricketer who is prepared to get down and work at the game.

The explanation is surely not far to seek. Batting, whether for a Test Match player or for a member of a junior school team, can consist of playing one ball at a time. To do this successfully a batsman must do three things: first, he must sight the ball; second, he must judge its length and decide what stroke he will play to it; and third, he must play that stroke correctly.

If to sight a cricket ball early and accurately is mainly a matter of the providential gift which we call 'ball sense', it should surely be assisted by correct positioning of the head and by general body balance in the stance. Stroke judgment, too, though partly a gift, is largely a matter of experience, though a coach can do something to help develop it in a boy in the nets and in discussion. But when we come to the actual stroke, we are concerned simply with a physical movement, the correct reflex response of the body to the brain's message. **This reflex response can only be achieved by constant practice: the body, in fact, must be 'grooved' to carry out automatically the right physical movement, and this is exactly what the activities of group coaching can and do achieve.** In them, for example, a batsman can in ten minutes play more off-drives to a ball dropped or tossed to the correct spot for that stroke than he might have the chance of playing in a whole afternoon of net practice. Thus gradually the stroke becomes grooved, and when next time out in the middle his mind telegraphs 'off-drive', his body will increasingly respond as it should.

The 'robot' criticism is frankly nonsense; batsmen will always vary according to their physical make-up, their natural gifts, their personal temperament: one boy's approach will be instinctively aggressive, another's defensive: one will naturally tend to play off the front foot and with plenty of top hand, another off the back with the right hand largely in control:

one will be ready and able to 'go down the track', another will tend to play 'on the crease', but whatever their natural resources and their basic approach, Group Coaching can help them to make the most of them.

Many of the distinguished players who have attended courses for the M.C.C. Advanced Coaching Certificate have volunteered their conviction that not only is group practice of high value as basic training for stroke production but that they themselves have even profited by it in their own play. Similar tribute is paid by many of those who have attended the consistently over-subscribed M.C.C. courses for Public, Grammar and Preparatory schoolmasters; they have found Group Coaching pays a real dividend at all levels of their school cricket, not only in terms of analysis, understanding and technique, but also in active enjoyment and sense of achievement.

The principles, whether of batting, bowling or fielding, which the coach should teach, have been set forth in the various chapters of this book, and it is here assumed that he has tried to study and master them. **He must all along try to explain 'why' as well as 'how'**, e.g. why the bat must be as long as possible on the line of the ball; why the position of the head and left shoulder, the movement of the feet, the control by the left wrist, matter in batting; why the bowler must keep sideways, use his body and follow-through; why the fielder must stoop early and keep his head down – and so on.

He should encourage his boys to ask questions in order to ensure that they really understand both the 'how' and the 'why'. In time he may even be able to single out one or two who can help him as 'junior coaches': incidentally, the ability in a boy to spot and to analyse another's faults in technique can be a great asset in improving his own.

As in all class-instruction there must be discipline and concentration and the coach must try to be as 'hundred-eyed as Argus' to mark what is done amiss. **But he must always remember that for the young 'practice' is to some extent an unsatisfactory preliminary to 'the real thing',** and he must ring the changes between, on the one hand, spells of 'stroke-grooving' with and without a ball and training in the pure technique of bowling and fielding and, on the other, competitions and 'match practice' on the lines that will later be suggested. **Above all there must be good humour and encouragement and at the end of every session the coach and his boys should feel that they have really 'got somewhere'.**

EQUIPMENT

Group Coaching demands a certain amount of equipment, but not more than the initiative of games masters and the co-operation of boys should be able to provide. The following are suggestions which can no doubt be improved and extended with experience.

Alan Knott. One more victim: there is the maximum economy of movement

Godfrey Evans. The ball was hooked to the boundary but, had it been missed, the wicket-keeper was ideally placed, with both feet and hands right over the line

Group Coaching. Learning to bowl starting from the second position in the Basic Action

Group Coaching. Practising the drive off the front foot in small groups

128d

Bats

A number of bats are necessary and it is very important that there should be a sufficient variety of sizes to cater for all their users: no boy can hope to derive benefit from practice, even from group practice without a ball, if he is using too big a bat. But given encouragement and the provision of a scale model on paper, the coach will find that boys can manufacture for themselves quite tolerable practice bats from soft wood which will serve the purpose for 'grooving the strokes' and for actually playing them against rubber balls. A more advanced practice bat, which can be used with harder balls, is now being turned out by the trade at a very moderate cost.

The following table records the dimensions and average weight of the various sizes of bats which are manufactured and suggests the approximate age for which each will normally be found suitable, though, of course, the determining factor in each case will be height and strength. A serviceable test is a boy's ability to swing and control the bat reasonably with the top end alone. It is always better for the bat to be too light than too heavy.

APPROXIMATE DIMENSIONS OF BATS

Size of bat	Length of bat in.	Length of handle in.	Width of blade in.	Weight lb.	oz.	Height of user
FULL SIZE	35	12	$4\frac{1}{4}$	2	4	5' 9" plus
SHORT HANDLE	34	11	$4\frac{1}{4}$	2	4	5' 7"– 5' 9"
HARROW	34	11	$4\frac{1}{4}$	2	3	5' 5"– 5' 7"
6	33	$10\frac{3}{4}$	4	2	2/1	5' 2"– 5' 5"
5	$31\frac{1}{2}$	$10\frac{3}{4}$	4	2	0	5' 1"– 5' 2"
4	$30\frac{1}{4}$	$10\frac{1}{2}$	$3\frac{7}{8}$	1	$8\frac{1}{2}$	5' 1"– 4' 7"
3	26	9	$3\frac{1}{4}$	1	2	below 4' 7"

Cricket Balls

Proper cricket balls should when possible always be used for bowling and batting practice, but their life on hard surfaces tends to be short and there are a number of relatively cheap and efficient types of composition balls on the market. It is important that small boys should not be allowed to practise or play with the full-sized ball; smaller and lighter balls ($4\frac{1}{4}$ and 4 ounces respectively) are now manufactured, and school authorities are increasingly concerned to reach agreement on the best size in different age groups. The plastic 'gamester' ball has been found valuable for indoor practice for all attacking strokes; these balls can be hit very hard without danger to windows or players. Although solid rubber balls of the lacrosse type, and tennis balls are normally used indoors for practising the defence strokes, they can be used for driving if the gymnasium has no low windows.

For outdoor practice on hard surfaces, lacrosse or tennis balls are the best, both for attacking and defending strokes.

The wicket

Several portable wickets will be needed: these are best provided in the form of a wooden base 11 in by 3 in by 3 in into which stumps are inserted or a plywood board of the correct width and height: if the stumps are painted on the latter so much the better. The base can profitably be stabilized by two metal bars, approximately 18 in long, 1½ in wide and ¼ in thick, secured at right angles to its length: but this is not necessary. Wickets can also usefully be chalked or painted on convenient walls.

The pitch

There should always be available a cord, knotted or in some way marked, to define 22 yds. Other knots 12 and 14 ft from one end will help in marking out the area for 'length targets'. Another useful adjunct will be a lath 6 to 7 ft in length and clearly marked as follows:

At   9 in – for the width of the wicket ⎫ for use when the wicket
At 28 in – for the height of the wicket ⎬ is to be chalked on a wall.
At 48 in – for the popping crease.

The full length of the lath will be used to mark out the continuation of the line of each stump beyond the popping crease.

Length targets

These are best provided in the form of thin tin plates, at least 3 ft by 2 ft: the tin, when struck, makes a satisfactory noise. Alternatively, plywood can be used, or the target can be chalked on the gymnasium floor or playground by filling in the area within a plywood frame.

Catching aids

Slip-cradles, of course, are excellent, but they are expensive and heavy to move about. The ordinary curved-topped dustbin can, with a tennis ball, provide very useful practice for quick reaction to catches at close range. The fielders should form a circle, standing at just more than full arm stretch from each other and with a radius of 3 or 4 yds from the bin. The new plastic spring-board screen provides excellent and enjoyable practice.

Hanging balls

Profitable use can be made of balls wrapped in rag or net and suspended by string from a beam or the ordinary horizontal bar in a gymnasium or a specially constructed T-shaped upright. The ball should hang some 4 to 6 in from the ground. This can be very helpful in grooving both the forward- and back-stroke and in teaching the boy really to watch the ball. The batsman's position will depend on whether he is playing the forward- or the back-stroke.

There is no substitute for constant practice and the coach should try to provide his boys with all the facilities he can for it, whether in the form of an adequate supply of bats and balls readily available, or permanent marks in the shape of wickets and length-targets at which they can bowl.

BATTING

Practice without the ball

With real beginners the initial stage of group coaching must take the form of demonstration, and practice without a ball, of the basic strokes. The coach must so align his class, whether on the playground, in the gymnasium or on the field, that they are safely clear of each other whatever they do with the bat, and can all get a clear view of him as he demonstrates. He will play each stroke successively facing his class, sideways to it, but especially away from it as in this position he can most easily be copied. Lines should be drawn in chalk or whitewash to represent the popping crease for each boy and another at right angles to it running back 48 in to where the leg stump would be: this will ensure that he takes up a correct stance and will also guide him in the straight back-lift (p. 77). It will also show him, when he comes to the back-stroke, how much room he has for stepping back.

The coach will explain to his boys the vital importance of the grip, stance and back-lift for all batting and will carefully check each boy's performance. He will then pass on to the mechanism of the forward- and back-strokes in that order. He will first demonstrate each stroke as it is played to the straight, the off and the leg ball and then drill his class in those movements. **At each stage he will explain 'the why' as well as 'the how',** invite questions and correct individual faults: **he must be especially on the watch against the tendency to get into tense and rigid attitudes, for if this becomes a habit, it will prevent free movement and timing when the ball comes into play. He must impress on the boys that in these 'drill' movements it is essential that they must each time imagine a bowler and a particular ball**

being bowled to them; if this is not done they may well forget that watching the ball is the pre-condition of any effective stroke.

On no account must the coach over-prolong this 'drill' stage: as soon as he feels that the boys have more or less grasped the basic technique of the stroke, he must get on to the essential and far more satisfying sequel of practice with the ball.

He will, of course, tell his boys that they cannot expect to get any stroke, or indeed any 'skill' in the game, 'grooved' in a single group practice. They must be prepared to work at them in their free time in pairs or small groups, criticising and helping each other: obviously, the more the coach can supervise and guide such individual practice the better.

The forward-stroke

For group practice, indoors or on asphalt playgrounds, solid rubber balls are best, but old tennis balls are adequate: on grass cheap composition balls can be used.

The class is now split into groups of three. The batsmen will stand 6 to 9 ft apart along the same parallel line on the edge of the practice area: the bowlers will stand 4 to 5 yds in front of them and the fielders rather nearer in the position of short-mid-off or short-mid-on. Three circles, about 1 ft in diameter, will be marked – in chalk if the surface is asphalt or wood, in whitewash if it is turf – about 6 to 8 in in front of the bat where it would finish in an ordinary defensive stroke played by a boy of average size: one will be in front of the middle stump, one 6 in outside the off stump and the third 6 in outside the leg stump. These are the bowlers' targets at which they direct the ball in an under-hand lob in order that the batsman may practise the ordinary forward-stroke (Fig. 1, page 134).

Alternatively, a single circle can be used and the batsman can shift his original stance to bring the target on to the off or on side of the wicket. Small boys will need to 'take guard' nearer the target, tall ones slightly farther away.

The practice will be in spells, first to the straight ball, then to the off ball and finally to the leg ball, the fielder, of course, shifting his position according to the line of attack (Fig. 1).

Every boy will take his turn as batsman, bowler or fielder in each spell.

Much practice is necessary with each kind of ball, straight, off and leg. Before every spell the coach will once again demonstrate the stroke, this time with the ball, and remind his class of its basic features: he will not hesitate, if necessary, to interrupt the ball practice and revert to the mechanics of the stroke without a ball until he is sure that they have been really understood.

The success of the whole activity depends so largely on the accuracy with which the ball is dropped on the target that the coach may well find it good economy to give his class a separate practice in this under-hand bowling before the stroke-play lessons start; the ball must be lobbed to a height of about 6 ft. If it is made competitive such practice can be quite fun.

The batsman can be given more advanced practice using all three targets and the bowler varying his line of direction from ball to ball: in this case there will be work for two fielders and the batsmen should be more widely spread. The coach must impress on the boys how much they can improve their fielding if they are alert and clean-handed even on this miniature scale.

The back-stroke

For the practice of back play the general disposition will be the same as for the forward-stroke, but the targets for the bowlers must be shortened to a line about 6 ft in front of the crease and the trajectory of the ball should be faster and lower: they may find it easier to throw the ball, and must try to keep the trajectory reasonably low and flat, perhaps by kneeling, or sitting.

As with the forward-stroke, the line of attack must be varied in spells, straight, to the off and to the on. In more advanced practice the bowler can vary the direction from ball to ball but in this case he should give the batsman a little more time for his stroke by bowling from rather farther away.

The drives

The drive, whether straight, to the off or to the on, is really only an extension and acceleration of the forward-stroke: once a boy has learnt how to play forward, he should be taught to drive, for until he can do so he can be immobilized by the bowler who keeps the ball well up to him. **Moreover it is the most exhilarating stroke in cricket and no part of group practice will pay a bigger dividend in enjoyment and in a feeling of achievement.**

Naturally, practice of the drives needs more space and more careful organization than the ordinary forward-stroke, but the following technique will be found both practicable and stimulating:

Each 'bowler' has a 'feeder' who stands behind him to collect the balls as they are rolled back to him by the fielders.

The 'bowler' stands about 2½ ft in front of and on the off side of the batsman so that the ball when dropped from his hand fully outstretched will fall just in front of the batsman's left foot at the end of a full forward stride. The batsman drives the ball on the second half-volley, i.e. just after it touches the ground on the second bounce (Fig. 2).

By altering the angle of his stance relative to the line of the dropped ball and by a slight adjustment on the part of the 'bowler', the batsman can practise the off and on drive just as effectively as he can the straight one (Figs. 1 and 2).

Fig. 1. Forward defence   *Fig. 2. The drives*

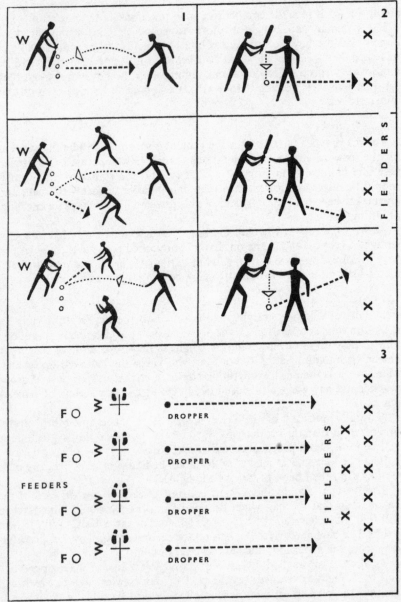

Fig. 3. The layout of a class for the straight drive

Fig. 4. All the drives   *Fig. 5. Hits to leg*

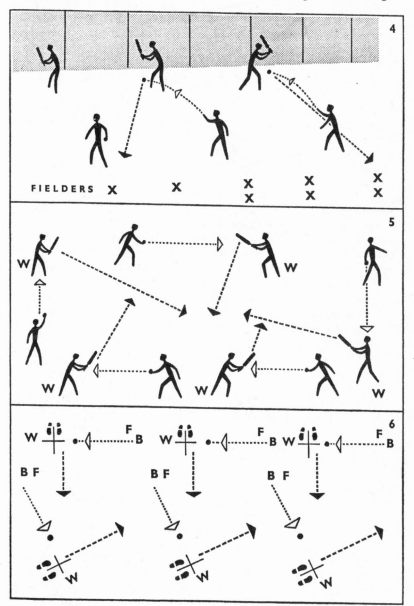

FIELDERS

Fig. 6. Square-cut   B—*bowler*   F—*feeder*

The quick-footed drive, played with a glide out to the pitch of the ball, can be practised in the same way, but in this case the 'bowler's' stance will be some 5½ ft in front of the batsman and he will drop the ball from a greater height, thus giving the batsman time to glide out to it.

This driving practice with sold rubber or tennis balls can provide admirable fun and training for a line of fielders stationed some 20 or 25 yds away (Fig. 3).

The larger the number of balls available for each 'bowler's' magazine, the more concentrated the practice. Batsmen, bowlers and fielders will, of course, need to change their roles in spells. Fielders should roll the ball back slowly to the bowlers' 'feeders'.

Where a tennis net is available, more advanced practice is possible. With the bowler bowling the ball from behind it to a batsman some 8 to 10 yds away the batsman drives the ball into the net. This has the advantage of demanding from the latter some judgment of flight, but it also demands some accuracy on the part of the bowler, especially for the practice of the quick-footed drive when he will have to bowl the ball higher and drop it shorter than for the one-stride drive. To minimize any chance of accident from mishits the pairs of bowlers and batsmen should be stationed well apart from each other. This practice can also be carried out indoors by using 'Gamester' balls, the batsmen arranged along the side of the room and the bowlers lobbing the ball under arm for straight, off- and on-drives. According to where the ball pitches the batsman will apply either the one-stride drive or the drive following the stride out (Fig. 4).

Finally, boys should be shown how they can practise driving by themselves by tossing up the ball with their left hand and then driving it into a net or against a wall.

With 'Gamester' balls indoors, or with tennis or solid rubber balls on outdoor hard surfaces, the practice of the lofted drive is both possible and valuable. The coach should impress upon his boys that if bowlers persist in dispensing with deep-fields they can be so driven with impunity and great profit.

Attacking back-strokes

With the use of the 'Gamester' balls the practice of the attacking back-stroke should present no difficulty. The layout will be the same as for the defensive back-stroke but the bowler should bowl or throw the ball rather faster and shorter than for normal back play and the fielder should be farther away: the line of the ball should be varied in spells from off to leg. Common faults in forcing back play are the same as in ordinary back play, but in the former the tendency for the right hand to take charge and drag the bat across the line must be especially watched. The left shoulder must be kept pointing down the line of the intended stroke. If the ball is forced to the off, the back of the left shoulder should face down the pitch.

Hitting to leg

The hitting of long-hops and full-pitches to leg may well prove the most profitable, as it certainly is an easy, phase of group coaching in batting; this is particularly true for beginners and small boys.

Batsmen and bowlers will be in one straight line, the batsmen standing with their backs and the bowlers with their right side to a fence, wall or net, if such is available; in the case of a fence or wall they should be at least 20 yds away from it: where there is none, fielders must be stationed at least 40 yds back in the square-leg area and should find themselves getting valuable practice in their own departments.

The bowlers will bowl full-pitches and long-hops in separate spells at and outside the batsman's legs, and the batsman will practise hitting them on the lines analysed on pp. 92–96. Indoors this stroke can be practised with 'Gamester' balls. A suggested layout is shown (Fig. 5), but care must be taken that batsmen have room to do their practice for each stroke otherwise if the room is crowded someone may be hit by a bat.

The cuts

As with the hits to leg, all the cuts can, since the advent of the 'Gamester' ball, be practised indoors. The 'bowling' (throwing) needs to be fast and accurate. Despite the fact that the cut off the front foot is rarely seen now in first-class cricket, it is certainly a stroke that pays dividends in school and club cricket and should be encouraged.

Suggested layouts are: there should be four in each group, batsman, bowler, a feeder to the bowler, and a wicket-keeper standing in first slip position. The bowler throws the ball at a chalked target and on a line about 9 or 10 ft away from the batsman between himself and the wicket-keeper to ensure that the direction and bounce is right for the shot to be played. For the cut off the front foot the ball should be shorter and wider than off the back foot (Fig. 6).

BOWLING

Whereas a good deal of group-coaching practice in batting may seem to boys some degrees removed from 'the real thing', this is much less true of bowling. But here too the foundations must be laid by explanation, demonstration and 'drill practice' of the correct bowling action.

The positions or stages of this action have been analysed on pp. 33–36. The coach will explain and demonstrate them by himself (without a ball) facing his class, sideways to it and especially, because this makes imitation easiest, away from it. In the case of small boys who are virtually starting

Fig. 7. The beginner's position

from scratch, possibly the best way of giving them the idea of rhythm in the delivery stride and of the importance of getting and keeping the body sideways is to place them in Position 3 of the basic actions (Fig. 7).

From this delivery stride position they should be taught to rock their weight backwards and forwards, back on to the right foot with the left arm swinging up and the right arm down (virtually into Basic Position 2) and then forward on to the left foot with the right arm swinging up and the left arm out and down (virtually Basic Position 4). When they have grasped and practised this movement they should be given a ball and told to start bowling on exactly the same lines, at a wicket-target, at a suitable short range. At this stage the coach should emphasize the vital importance of looking, and thinking where they want to bowl, and of the follow-through into Position 5.

The next step is to preface them with the run-up: for small boys this should never be more than 6 to 8 yds and the coach should emphasize that it must be uniform and regular, smooth and gradually accelerating. A common fault is to begin to run up too fast too early.

When the run-up has been welded on to the action, the boy is ready to begin regular bowling practice at full range for which he is qualified by this age and strength, in the case of beginners probably somewhere between 12 and 16 yds.

This practice should always be carried out with the incentive of a wicket to bowl at and a length target, either a good sized sheet of tin or a hoop, and if it is made competitive, so much the better.

The coach should preface every practice by emphasizing how important it is, if he is to hope for any accuracy, that throughout the whole bowling action the bowler's head should be kept as level and still as possible, and that in the last stride or two of his run-up the eyes and the mind should be fixed on the spot where he intends to drop the ball.

When he is satisfied that they have grasped the principles of the action, in fact when they have got the feeling of how they want to bowl, he can start on the real job of teaching how to command length and direction.

For group practice with the ball the coach will divide his class into pairs of teams. The size of each team must depend on the space and the number of wickets available: it may have to be as large as nine, but four is a good working unit. There will be a wicket at each end of the pitch (21 yds for the twelve-to-fourteens and correspondingly shorter for younger boys). A target, preferably of tin, at least 3 ft by 2 ft, will be placed crosswise with its near edge about 10 ft in front of each wicket. The teams will line up 7 or 8 yds behind and on the leg side of their wicket: team A will then bowl in turn at their target, each boy after bowling going to the end of the bowling queue, whilst team B, similarly relieve each other in the post of wicket-keeper. It will save time if each of the bowling team has a ball and if the stumper, as he takes it, throws it to the end of his own team's queue to build up their 'magazine'. When all team A have bowled, team B take over from their end. If enough balls for this are not available, one can be used, the teams bowling alternate balls.

When every boy of both teams has bowled an over, the target can be turned round so that it lies not crosswise but head-on to the pitch, thus putting a premium on accuracy of direction.

This team bowling practice should always be competitive, five points being assigned for a ball that pitches on the tin, five for one that hits the wicket (ten for 'the double') and two forfeited for every ball to leg.

A more elaborate competitive bowling practice can be run by marking out a ground target as shown on the following page.

The line A-B represents the near minimum for a length ball: its distance from the wicket E-F will, of course, vary with the average age and pace of the boys bowling. For medium-paced bowlers of fourteen and upwards this line may be drawn at 13 ft from the stumps: for younger or slower bowlers it should be 1 ft or 18 in nearer to them.

The line D-C, drawn 3 ft nearer the wicket than A-B, marks the maximum limit for the length ball. Line G-H represents the popping-crease. Lines A-E and B-F define the direction target.

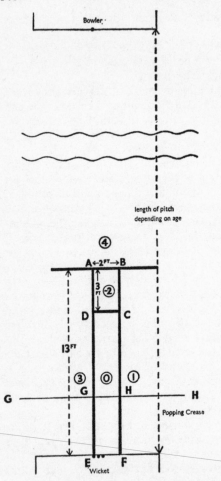

TARGET FOR TRAINING IN ACCURACY

The distance of the line AB from the bowling crease EF is shown as 13 ft – this distance must be adjusted to suit the age of the boys, and the nature of the wicket, to ensure that a ball of average pace pitching on the line AB is not short of a good length. When several boys are bowling, each must make a mental adjustment to suit the pace of his bowling.

For older boys, 13½ ft is generally regarded a good average distance on turf wickets.

The scale of scoring is shown on the plan by the figures in circles and aims at driving home the importance of length and direction and particularly the sin of bowling short or to leg.

A ball pitching short of A-B scores 4 against the bowler.

A ball pitching between A-B and G-H on the leg side of A-E scores 3 against him.

A ball pitching between A-B and G-H on the off side of B-F scores 1 against.

A ball pitching in the area D-C, G-H scores nought.

A ball pitching in the good length and direction area A-B, C-D gives him a credit of 2.

The object of the bowler is to forfeit the fewest points for one or more overs.

After some experiment coaches should be able to establish a 'standard', varying according to the boys' age and proficiency, and this should provide a further incentive for competitive practice. It may well be that in early stages an appreciably larger target may be found desirable to provide the necessary degree of encouragement.

FIELDING

In Chapter 1 the basic technique of fielding has been analysed and suggestions offered for normal methods of fielding practice: in themselves these are 'group activities', but they can be supplemented. Where there is a wall available, a line of wickets or of circles 2 ft in diameter with their bottom at the height of the bails, can be chalked on it some 8 or 10 ft apart and boys can practise throwing at these targets, gathering the rebound and throwing again. Their aim should be about a foot above the wicket or the top half of the circle: solid rubber balls are best for this purpose but tennis balls will do. The range will, of course, vary according to the age and proficiency of the class, but 15 ft would be about normal. This can be carried out either singly or in groups of two, each fielding and returning the rebound from the other's throw: they should interchange at intervals so that each will have practice with the ball as it would come to him on the off and on side. This is valuable exercise not only for accuracy of throwing but for quickness of footwork and stooping in taking the rebound cleanly.

Another throwing competition which boys enjoy has a central 'wicket' which serves as a target for three or four couples disposed as in the diagram on p. 142.

Each couple has a ball which they throw alternately at the target wicket, counting five points for a hit.

Any three sticks of approximately the size of a stump will do for the target and they should be so arranged in a triangle so that roughly the same width of the target presents itself to any angle of attack.

Here again the range will be elastic, but a circle with a ten-yard radius would be a reasonable basis for experiment.

Wicket-keepers can get excellent practice if they can get two friends to come with them, one to throw the ball from a range of about 12 to 15 yds and the other, with a bat, to play at, miss or occasionally hit it. There should always be a wicket or something to represent one and the keeper should concentrate on vigilance, footwork, taking the ball correctly, and bringing it back to the stumps.

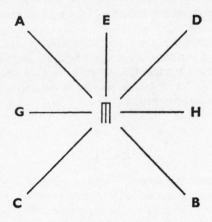

CIRCULAR CRICKET

This is a half-way house to match play proper and is of high value in providing the maximum of continuous and varied activity for every boy. It is most conveniently played in groups of nine with the following layout:

(9) Padding up.

(6) Slip or gully.

(2) Wicket-keeper.

(5) Cover-point.   (1) Batsman.   (7) Square-leg.

(3) Bowler.

(4) Mid-off.   (8) Mid-on.

Play on these lines for four or five minutes, according to total time available, and then change round clockwise, wicket-keeper to batsman, batsman to square-leg, square-leg to mid-on, mid-on to bowler, etc.: No. 9 comes in to bat and slip pads up. Continue thus till every boy has batted, bowled, kept wicket and fielded in every position.

THE ORGANIZATION OF A CRICKET 'GAMES-LESSON'

In Group Coaching the aim of the games master will always be to provide as continuous, varied and satisfying activity as possible for every boy. Though the average boy loves to play and tends to find practice irksome, he must be persuaded that only by 'going through the mill' of practice can he hope to reach the top. **At the same time his natural enthusiasm must be sustained by as much match play or at least 'match practice' as possible.**

The organization of a coaching lesson will necessarily depend on the number of boys involved and the time and playing space available: games masters will be able to make their own adjustments and probably improvements on the following suggested schedule for an hour's lesson at the start of the season for a class of some forty boys.

First half hour

Practice of 'skills' in six groups each of 6 to 8 boys.

First ten minutes

Groups A and B – batting
Groups C and D – bowling
Group E   – target fielding   ⎱ 5 minutes each and
Group F   – cradle or dustbin catching ⎰ interchange.

Second ten minutes

Groups E and F – batting
Groups A and B – bowling
Groups C and D – fielding and catching – 5 minutes each.

Third ten minutes

Groups C and D – batting
Groups E and F – bowling
Groups A and B – fielding and catching – 5 minutes each.

Second half hour

All groups engage in circular cricket as already described.

It is important to ensure that in any one week every boy has at least one practice at each of the group 'skills'. As the season goes on, the amount of time devoted to these will diminish in favour of 'match practice'. In the early stages the games master will find his cricket problem appreciably helped if the 'skills' first explained and demonstrated can be practised as part of the general activities of the physical training lesson.

This lesson can be likened to a meccano building set, the pieces of which consist of:

(a) Drill of strokes without the ball.

(b) Practice of strokes using the ball.

(c) Practices of the various other 'skills' of cricket – bowling, fielding, catching, throwing, etc.

(d) Play in small groups – 'circular cricket'.

These pieces can be fitted together in many different ways resulting in each case in a 'complete' lesson. **In such a lesson all boys in the class would be actively engaged in practising some skill of cricket, or playing circular cricket. Drill, practices and play should be mingled, thus avoiding any suggestion of monotony.**

9

The Choice and Care of Equipment

In the Long Room at Lords there are preserved many bats of historic
interest, ranging from the curved and blackened veteran of the eighteenth
century to one used by Sir Donald Bradman on his last tour of England.
Each in its time has been the personal and prized possession of some
cricketer, and for every boy today, as he grows into the game, his bat is,
or should be, part of his cricketing self, and its choice and care a matter
of real concern.

In its selection a boy will be well advised to invite the advice of an
experienced cricketer. With bats now costing more than twice as much as
they did a generation ago, there is a natural temptation to advise a boy to
choose a bat into which he will 'grow', but the price of such economy may
be high, for his batting method may be fatally warped by using a bat
which is either too big or too heavy.

Given that it is of the right size, the most important considerations are
its balance and its 'drive'. Balance is far more important than weight on
the scales, and between two bats of the same weight there may be a vital
difference in 'pick up'. A well-balanced bat should lift easily and yet give
the feeling that there is some 'body' in it as it comes into the stroke. The
'drive' of a bat depends on the resilience of its handle, the quality of its
willow and the amount of wood in the driving part. Given that the general
weight and balance of the bat is right, the more wood there is in the blade
the better. Most modern handles have the right resilience: this can readily
be tested by placing the left hand at the top of the handle, the right hand at
the bottom, and then, with the foot of the blade on the ground, bringing
all the weight of the body to bear on the right hand: it should be possible
to feel a definite give in the handle. The best willow, which comes from the
heart of the tree, is straight grained: these grains may vary in number from
five to twelve or even fifteen in the face of the blade: there is no golden rule
but the more uniform the spacing of the grain the better, and very broad-
grained bats sometimes tend to go 'sullen': the only real test of a bat's
drive is with a ball: the response of a really good blade is unmistakable in
its liveliness, at once sweet and crisp.

The bat once selected, there is a good deal to be said for having its blade
reinforced about an inch from the foot by a very narrow strip of fine binding, for this is some insurance against the blade splitting, e.g. in contact

with a fast yorker, before it is really broken in. The blade of a new bat should be well oiled before use with raw linseed oil, but care should be taken to keep the oil off the splice. Boys tend to over-oil their bats; too much oil will do more harm than good, for it tends to clog the bat face. Once a bat is driving well, the important thing is to keep the face clean with sandpaper and to confine the oiling to an occasional wipe-over with an oily rag. Should the face at any time appear to have become clogged and the bat to have lost life, this oil-veneer should be carefully scraped off with a safety razor blade: in extreme cases of hardness the grains can be very slightly opened by running the point of the blade down them. Bats must on no account be allowed to become wet: they should never be left to lie on damp turf and, if rained upon, should be wiped dry as soon as possible.

New bats must be broken-in discreetly: the best way to start is by knocking up an old ball on them, and it is as well where possible to postpone the first use of a new bat, whether at a net or in the middle, until a reasonably warm and dry day arrives.

Cracks on the edge should be sealed at once with surgical tape; more serious damage may demand glueing and binding with twine, but this inevitably affects the weight and the pick up.

All bats today are sold with rubber handles: these often tend to work loose, in which case they must be at once reglued, for a loose handle may very easily and fatally betray a stroke.

Careful investigation and experiment has recently led to an extension of the variety of sizes of pads for boys and it should now be possible for any boy to be properly suited: the correct fitting of the knee is the acid test. Maximum protection must not be sought at the expense of comfort and mobility. Pad straps are generally made unnecessarily long and should be cut down so that only an inch or so will overlap the buckle: a cricketer should take proper pride in keeping his pads clean.

Whether in practice or in the middle a boy should always, if he has them, wear two batting gloves. The best protection is provided by those of tubular rubber, but the majority of gloves today are of the horse-hair stuffed type: these are either made with finger stalls and open palms or as gauntlets with a leather or cotton grip. Choice is a matter of taste; many batsmen prefer the open variety as giving them a better feel of the handle, but those whose palms sweat freely prefer the gauntlet: the drawback to this latter is that the gauntlet grip tends to wear out rather quickly and demands renewal. A 'protector' is a great reinforcement to a batsman's confidence, and may well save him from crippling injury: if he has a protector, he should never bat without it.

His footwear is really the most important part of a cricketer's equipment, for it conditions the footwork and balance on which all bowling, batting and fielding depend. Rubber soles can only grip dry ground and for all conditions there is no substitute for properly studded leather: boots are always preferable to shoes, especially for bowlers, as providing better ankle support. Every cricketer who means business will keep a close watch on his studs to see that none are missing and that they are not clogged up with mud. On wet ground bowlers may well take a knife into the field – and if it has a hoof-pick all the better – which they can use as necessary to clean their studs of mud: they should do the same at any interval. Dirty boots are the sign of a slovenly cricketer. A pair of bootbags in linen or hessian are very useful in keeping the dirt on boots away from flannels in the cricket bag.

A cricketer's wardrobe will, of course, be conditioned by his purse, but certain general aims may be suggested. A sweater is most desirable, above all for bowlers, who will be wise, even in warm weather, to put it on at the end of each bowling spell and, if it is at all cold, between overs. Many batsmen like to keep their sweaters on when they first go in: warmth is certainly essential if the muscles are to respond quickly and some find that it also helps their nerves. But even if he is not making runs, a batsman very soon warms up at the crease and the sweater should then be discarded. Fielders, too, must keep warm and it is far better to go out in a sweater than to wish one had. A spare shirt, if available, should always be taken to a cricket match, for if a player has really sweated it will save him from stiffness or even a chill. If he has an old pair of trousers, he can use them for batting and so save his best pair for fielding until in course of time they qualify for the other role.

Socks, though unseen, are not the least important part of the outfit and they should be thick: many players, specially bowlers, like to wear two pairs and choose their boots to fit accordingly: this certainly saves the feet on hard grounds and no one can do himself justice if his feet are blistered and sore. A change of socks after a long spell in the field or a long innings is wonderfully refreshing. Most cricketers today like to play in caps and the modern cap is well cut, though a word of caution is needed against the oversized peak which may interfere with the line of sight. Those who prefer to play bare-headed should make certain that their hair is not so long as to get into their eyes!

In these days of mounting prices, cricket balls, whether private or club property, must more than ever be well looked after: they must never be allowed to lie out in the rain and if they do become wet or muddy after use at the nets or in fielding practice, they, and especially their seams, should be cleared of all mud with a damp rag, then wiped over with another that has a suspicion of oil on it and then allowed to dry naturally. It is wonderful how the life and the attractive appearance of a ball can be preserved with proper care, and how soon neglect can transform it into something seamless, slippery and irresponsive.

A final word may be said on the winter storage of cricket equipment.

Bats should be lightly oiled before being put away and should be kept in as equable a temperature as possible. Boots or shoes, especially their soles, should be thoroughly cleaned before being put away. For flannels not in winter use moth balls are a good insurance.

It is most important as a safeguard against rotting that all netting, and matting where used, should be completely dried out before being stored. A slip-cradle must, of course, be brought under cover and a thin coating of oil be put on its ribs.

10

Grounds and Pitches

There are all too few cricket grounds in this country for the boys who want to play cricket, and on all too many of them the condition of the pitches and of the out-field is such as not only to affect their pleasure in playing but also to make it very difficult for them really to learn the game.

The great batsman may triumph over a difficult wicket, the great fielder may, even on a rough ground, pick up cleanly most balls that come to him, but only too often the young cricketer can be fatally and finally discouraged by the conditions under which he plays. However much and however good the coaching he may get, he cannot be expected to 'keep his nose down' in batting if the length ball or even the half-volley may get up and hit him in the mouth, or to watch the ball until the last moment in ground fielding if the same thing may happen to him. If any coaching campaign is to bear as much fruit as it might, more and better grounds and, above all, more and better pitches, **especially practice pitches,** must be forthcoming.

The provision of new grounds and of the staff and equipment necessary for the proper maintenance of those that already exist is a matter for the public authorities, whether educational or municipal: so in the main is the problem of laying down artificial pitches, whether for match or practice. Of this nothing will be said here except to emphasize the immense value to he coach of even one such practice pitch with a really true playing surface as distinct from the rough and often dangerous turf wickets on which only too often he has to try to teach his boys to bat.

The object of this chapter is to offer some suggestions for the upkeep of grounds and the preparation of turf wickets. The resources both in equipment and in labour available will, of course, differ widely, though it is here suggested for official consideration that a generous outlay in equipment will not only make an immense difference to playing conditions but may well prove a profitable investment in the saving of labour-cost. Even where these resources are most meagre, it is hoped that much of the programme suggested will be found practicable and **those who try to follow it can at least be sure that, however short of their aim the results of their efforts may fall, the boys who play on their grounds will have good cause to be grateful for them.**

149

THE RECOVERY OF THE OUT-FIELD

(Note: it is assumed throughout that football is played over the out-field, possibly late into March: even where this is not the case, the same programme will hold good except that there will be less need of 'spike-harrowing').

(i) As soon as football is over, sow really bare areas with a mixture containing 50 per cent of Rye Grass (viz.: S23 or Kentish Indigenous): this will germinate more rapidly than the finer grasses. The goal area of football grounds should, if possible, be re-turfed, but in a dry spring, especially if winds are cold, this turf will need watering: re-seeding is a poor alternative and not a great deal cheaper.

(ii) When the ground is reasonably dry, use a light spike-harrow and then distribute the 'crumbs' with a brush-harrow or wire drag pulled all ways. An efficient substitute can be found in a roll of disused wire-netting.

(iii) 'Aerate' the ground as much as possible with a turf-piercing machine: most public authorities own them; so that it should at least be possible to borrow one. 'Turf, like men and animals, lives on oxygen and light'.

(iv) Rolling can now begin, but with a **light** roller; the heavy roller will follow but must never be used when the ground is wet as well as soft; to use it under these conditions may produce a superficially attractive surface but at the fatal price of forming an impenetrable roof through which the young grass cannot sprout and which, when it dries, will crack badly. No roller should ever be used when frost is coming out of the ground.

(v) During the season cut frequently, but not too close, with a gang-mower: the closer the cut, the more it takes out of the ground; provided that the gang-mower is used often enough, the cuttings may be left on the ground and will help to feed it. But unless a gang-mower is available for **frequent** use, i.e. at least once a week, a power-mower with box will more effectively check the spreading of weeds.

(vi) Spray with selective weed-killer when weeds are in full growth; this is generally in early June.

TREATMENT OF THE MATCH SQUARE AND NET WICKETS

(a) *Where football has been played*

(i) At the first showery spell from mid-March onwards, irrespective of football, distribute fertilizer over the area, scrupulously following manufacturer's instructions, and, unless there is rain, sprinkle it with water the next day.

(ii) As soon as the ground is reasonably dry, spike with machine and then rake by hand in both directions, i.e. north-south and east-west, ensuring that the tilth is spread over scars and hollows. If, however, the ground is **badly** cut up by football, additional tilth will have to be brought in from suitable and sifted top soil from the edge of the field. Distribute this and work it in with a 'straight-edge'.

(iii) Broadcast seed, working it into the tilth with a wooden rake or wire drag. Local seedsmen can be consulted as to the best mixture, but for quick restoration it should contain 50 per cent of the S.23 Rye Grass. This grass, though on the coarse side, will, if properly maintained, produce true and well-wearing wickets.

(iv) Put a very light roller, e.g. a hand-roller-mower with driving chain removed, over this seeded tilth and then leave it till the grass is $1\frac{1}{2}$ to 2 in high. This period will be about three weeks in the case of fine grass but with the Rye Grass mixture about ten days.

(v) Then start mowing but with the machine set high so as only to take off about half the grass growth: for this it is essential that the cutting blades should be really sharp.

(vi) Then start light rolling and, as the grass strengthens, cut lower.

(b) Where no football has been played

AT THE END OF THE CRICKET SEASON

 (i) Sow thin areas by 'pricking in' and cover with medium loam.

 (ii) Re-turf bowlers' holes at any time during the autumn, but when the ground is sufficiently wet for the turf 'to take'.

 (iii) Spray or 'spot-treat' the weeds with selective weed-killer at normal strength.

 (iv) Continue regular cutting till growth of grass stops.

IN AUTUMN OR EARLY WINTER

 (v) Aerate turf by turf-piercing machine or, if the square threatens to be very compact, do the same more closely by hand. Where a turf-piercer is not available and labour is short for hand-piercing, an adequate substitute for the former can be made by driving 3-in nails through a $\frac{1}{2}$-in board some 18 in long and 8 in broad, on top of which a second board of similar dimensions should be bolted with provision made for a central handle.

IN THE SPRING

 (vi) Provided that the ground is reasonably open, give it a dressing of fertilizer, e.g. sulphate of ammonia, in early April.

 (vii) Start rolling with a light hand-roller and then gradually increase the weight, but this general rolling must not be confused with the really heavy rolling which is the last stage in the preparation of a particular pitch for a match.

(viii) On any open, mild day, when worms are near the surface, de-worm with Mowrah meal: on some grounds it may be advisable to give them a second dose. When casts are dry, scarify with brush harrow or wire-netting drag.

(ix) Continue treatment as in (a) (v) above.

THE PREPARATION OF A PITCH FOR A MATCH

Starting some days before the match:

(i) Select the site and brush it well.

(ii) With a clean-cutting machine give it a double cut up and down the pitch, thus ensuring a uniform texture free from mowing streaks.

(iii) Water thoroughly with a sprinkler or hose pipe and rose to penetrate three inches according to the state of the ground. Surface watering with bucket and can, when water is not laid on, is dangerous: it may well produce a pitch off which the ball 'flies' even worse than off a hard ground.

(iv) Working from the edges to the middle, inspect the surface carefully, especially in the area of the length ball at each end, and where any indentations are seen lift them with a fine-pronged fork or knife and then tread them gently back to level out.

(v) When the grass surface is free from moisture – but not before – give it a first rolling: the heavier the roller used, the more necessary it is to wait till the moisture is out of the surface. This first rolling should be limited to producing a smooth face.

(vi) On the next day sprinkle with water unless rain has fallen, and then consolidate with the heavy roller. Repeat rolling on following days.

(vii) On the morning of the match give the pitch a final light brush and double cut with a mower set as close as possible. Give a final fifteen minutes' roll, mark out the creases and inspect the stumps.